Daddy and the Two Bears

Gary Anderson

3P
PUBLISHING

Copyright © 3P Publishing

First published in 2021 in the UK

3P Publishing

C E C, London Road
Corby
NN17 5EU

A catalogue number for this book is available from the British Library

ISBN 978-1-913740-17-7

Cover design: Marie-Louise O'Neill

I would like to dedicate this book to my wife Michelle (Shelly). To this day I still do not know how she does it. She has walked in front of me to guide me, she has walked behind me to stop me from falling and now she walks beside me. She has stood by me through everything. I will always be in debt to her as I wouldn't be here if it wasn't for her. She truly is an angel.

Love you always.

xxx

Foreword

In this heart-rending book, Gary Anderson takes us on an emotional journey that is often harrowing and challenging. Ultimately, though, it is an uplifting story of courage, fortitude and love, told with brutal honesty about his own inner struggles, yet with real tenderness towards his partner Michelle and their beloved twins, the 'Bears', Alana and Dana, this book serves as a beacon of hope for all of us.

Thank you, Gary.

Paul Whitehouse - actor, writer and comedian

Preface

It gives me great pleasure to write a preface for Gary Anderson's book relating to the personal journey of a couple through a complicated pregnancy, with which I was involved. He bravely focuses on the difficult experience of a monochorionic twin pregnancy, complicated by Twin to Twin Transfusion Syndrome (TTTS) and how it led to the sad loss of their daughters, Alana and Dana.

TTTS is a morbid disease that complicates 10% of all identical twin pregnancies. Although treatment strategies have altered since this pregnancy, it remains a disease that carries high fetal mortality. We are involved in managing approximately sixty pregnancies a year complicated by TTTS and strive to improve the outcomes in this complex disease. Healthcare professionals and carers of parents coping with such events and pregnancies are aware of the unremitting stress and emotion that couples experience, and that, sadly, some have to deal with bereavement at the end of the journey.

This moving book examines the bereavement and emotions of such a pregnancy and uniquely focuses on the emotion experienced by Gary and in the context of grief experiences by both him and Michelle, his wife. It is a testament to a couple's inner strength, but also a reminder to healthcare professionals that there is much more to the treatment of TTTS than the management of the clinical problem.

Mark Kilby, Professor of Fetal Medicine, Birmingham, UK

Preface

We first met Gary early in 2018 and were privileged to hear his story that has now been recounted in this book. Gary and his wife Michelle experienced a twin pregnancy that was complicated by Twin to Twin Transfusion Syndrome. This very sadly resulted in the loss of their daughters Alana and Dana.

Gary's openness and determination to share the enormous emotional demands of their journey and ultimately grieving for the loss of both daughters is very clear.

This exceptional account will help other families and professionals working with multiple birth families to understand the impact of an experience such as this on the whole family. Sadly, bereavement is more common in multiple pregnancies due to complications in the pregnancy and pre-term delivery.

About 32% of twins are born before thirty-two weeks gestation compared with about 1% of single babies and twins are about five times more likely to die in their first year.

Although there has been increased interest in parents' experiences in recent years, most of the publications focus solely on the mother. Whilst it is important that we understand the mother's perspective, this often means that the father's voice is unheard. When childbirth does not go according to plan, fathers often feel that they have to be strong in order to protect their partner and the rest of the family.

They may struggle to maintain a work/life balance, have to cope with unexpected financial pressures, face role uncertainty and feel powerless about the situation they suddenly find themselves in. These challenges are magnified if the birth involves twins or higher order multiples.

A key issue that men often report is that they did not have anyone with insight to their experiences with whom they could share their feelings either at the time or after the event. Gary's account from a personal perspective will have a huge impact and reach others in a way that other books can never achieve.

At the Elizabeth Bryan Multiple Births Centre, we will certainly be using the book in our education programme for professionals and to support other parents.

Jane Denton, Co-founder and co-lead, Elizabeth Bryan Multiple Births Centre, Birmingham City University, and Director, Multiple Births Foundation.
Merryl Harvey, Co-founder, Elizabeth Bryan Multiple Births Centre, Birmingham City University, formerly Professor of Nursing and Family Health, Birmingham City University

Preface

I remember Gary and Michelle from the time of their pregnancy with the girls, but they didn't stand out particularly. They were a lovely young couple going through a difficult time, like many other young couples I was used to seeing. It was on the day that the decision was made to deliver the twins that my first very clear memories start. We didn't have cots and therefore they needed to go to a different hospital for the delivery by Caesarean section on arrival.

My abiding memory of that afternoon was that of anger and frustration with the attitude of the two female ambulance crew who arrived to transport Michelle and Gary. They must be the two most unsympathetic and rude women ever to have been employed in a caring profession.

We had cared for and nurtured this young family and wanted to hand them over to people who were equally caring; we felt like parents sending our children into the abyss. Fortunately, the staff at the other hospital were a lot nicer than the ambulance crew.

Following the sad loss of their twin girls, we formed a relationship with almost the entire extended family. Michelle's family did lots of fundraising events for the department and Gary has done numerous heroic fundraisers on our behalf. Michelle is the epitome of calm and stoicism. She went on to have two successful pregnancies, always remembering her twin daughters and marking every anniversary and milestone event. Gary has risen like a phoenix from the fire; he has turned his life around as a result of losing his little daughters. The nice, ordinary dad I first knew has blossomed into one of the most impressive people I have ever had the privilege to know. He has retrained as a counsellor to support others who are feeling vulnerable and he has given so much back. He is a great husband and father.

I expect he will credit Michelle for his turnaround and she certainly has been a positive influence; but he must also take a huge amount of credit for the way he has conducted himself and what he has achieved in his life so far.

Finally, in 2017, he reached a point where he could look at the girl's memory boxes and allow himself the chance to cry. I believe that those two little girls would have been very proud of their fabulous dad.

Veronica Donovan OBE, Consultant Midwife in Fetal Medicine, Birmingham Women's and Children's Hospital

Abigail's Footsteps

We set up Abigail's Footsteps in 2010 after our daughter Abigail Ward was stillborn at 41 weeks gestation. We wanted to help other bereaved parents and in particular improve the way they are cared for when in hospital. Over the last 10 years, our charity has worked alongside midwives, NHS hospitals and specialist advisors across the UK to both raise awareness of stillbirth and find ways to better educate those involvement in working with bereaved parents. We have achieved a lot but sadly, stillbirth and neonatal deaths is a daily occurrence. Through our charity we provide counselling to parents, education to medical professionals and equipment to hospitals to help the many bereaved families come to terms with their sad loss.

Gary is kindly donating some of the money from this book to our charity as a way to help others that have gone or are going through a similar experience.

David and Jo Ward, Co-Founders of Abigail's Footsteps
www.abigailsfootsteps.co.uk

Author's introduction

It's difficult to know where to start. Where do you start when there's so much to tell? Where do you start when there are so many interwoven events and feelings, each playing their own, individual and important role in my story, yet unable to paint the whole picture without the support of each other? Spaghetti Junction has nothing on me.

Do I start by telling you about the Bears? Their mum? My mum? Me? And that's just for starters. What I will tell you, though, is that what you will read is the way I saw it, from my perspective, during some of the most traumatic events that anyone could possibly live through.

Even as a child, I had an image of what a dad should be like. I have no recollection of when I first thought that I wanted to be one, probably when I was in single figures and short trousers, I'd imagine. Why, I don't know. Maybe I wanted to be what my own dad wasn't. Then, like many others, as I matured and had relationships, I looked ahead to a future through rose-tinted glasses – mine would be the perfect family!

The family I wanted, and the type of dad that I looked up to and wanted to be, was one like *The Waltons* off the TV, or the Ingalls family from *Little House on the Prairie*. Those of you who are familiar with those two American series from the 1970s will know exactly what I mean, but for those who don't, theirs were families that stuck together, no matter what. Storylines covered alcoholism, poverty, prejudice, illness, blindness, racism – you name it. But the outcome was always the same: they pulled together when it counted. Mums and dads taught morals and ethics to the younger folk, and I yearned to be even a little part of that, to be a dad of the perfect family, just like the Waltons or the Ingalls.

Maybe I was living in cloud-cuckoo-land. TV and reality don't always go together. But never, as a boy, did I expect the future to be blighted by such sadness and sorrow that was never included in a script of *The Waltons* or *The Little House on the Prairie*.

This is my story.

1

'You don't have to do it if you don't want to, honestly,' said my wife, Michelle. 'If it's too much, then we'll just miss doing it this year.'

I'm sure she meant it, and she said it in a genuinely sympathetic and understanding way, but I knew how much me doing this meant to her and how important it was. It was coming up to our twins' birthday. Another year, another year older – but another year without them. For both of us, this was always the toughest part of our year.

In the twins' memory, Michelle had been delivering cakes to her close family every year to mark their birthday. She'd been doing it for years, but this year was different. Michelle was recovering from breast cancer surgery, and couldn't drive or even sit in the car for the duration of the drop-offs.

It had long since dawned on me that it was coming up to the 'cake run', but I'd tried to put it to the back of my mind, hoping almost that it would be forgotten about, with everything else that was going on with Michelle.

'No, no, I'll do it, if you really want me to,' I said, trying to disguise my reluctance. 'The kids'll want me to do it, too, so I'll do it.'

Shit! I'd committed to it now. I'd never done the cake run before, not been involved in the buying of the cakes or the drop-offs. I'd always avoided anything to do with the cakes. My choice. I didn't want to have anything to do with it; it was Michelle's thing, not mine.

As our two young kids had got older, they'd jumped in the car with Michelle and joined in the cake run with great enthusiasm. I'd never wanted to go with them. I'd wave them off, then breathe a sigh of relief that I wasn't involved, and busy myself around the house or elsewhere. They'd leave somewhere between 6am and 7am on the Sunday morning that fell before the twins' birthday, the kids still in their PJs, slippers and dressing gown.

There'd be a pile of fresh cream sponge cakes on the front passenger seat, all wrapped up, ready to be delivered to Michelle's family. They'd drop each cake off secretly on each doorstep, as Santa might leave Christmas presents, then leave without a trace. The kids loved it. It was exciting – and they got to have treats in the back of the car as Michelle drove to each destination. Easily pleased!

The whole trip took about an hour and a half, then they'd be home again, back on the drive, and our day would continue as normal. I'd always ask if it'd gone well, if anyone had heard them, if there was any traffic, and so on, but nothing more than that. Michelle bought a cake for us so that we, too, could remember the twins' birthday, of course. We'd have a slice after tea, and enjoy it – or maybe we'd pretend to a little.

This year the tradition was mine to fulfil, my first cake run. I could have said no, but I didn't. I wanted to do it for Michelle. She'd been doing it for so many years, and under all the circumstances that prevented her from doing it this year, it was the least I could do. I wanted to do it for the kids, too. They were expecting me to jump into Michelle's shoes and do what they did every year. Most importantly, I wanted to do it for the twins.

Little did I know that the experience of that day would prompt a sudden change in me. That very event, the carrying out of the cake run, would trigger an explosion of emotion that had been locked deep, deep, down inside me for many years. I thought I'd never, ever want it to come to the surface. In fact, I'd spend years using copious amounts of energy to make sure it was kept under wraps. But the eruption was just too strong to hold down any more.

On that day, the day of the cake run, I knew that I needed to tell my story.

2

The day I first met Michelle, back in 1999, I was complete mess. In fact, I was like a ticking bomb about to explode internally. My life was going nowhere, I was out of work having finished a close protection contract up in Scotland, didn't know where my next contracts were going to come from, and nor did I have a clue where I was going to live. The prospect of going overseas, an option that had been offered to me, seemed like a good one. It'd get me away from everyone, including myself – I'd had enough of what life had thrown me - and maybe someone might be kind enough to blow my head off if I became a mercenary.

A relationship I was in had recently gone to shite because of my erratic life and behaviour, and on that night, I was about to help an old boss beat the living daylights out of a group of drug dealers in a local pub. Instead, by pure chance, I met Michelle.

She was just out with a friend, dancing the night away. My old boss took a shine to her friend instead of what he'd really come for, and me and Michelle were left standing, wondering what to say to each other. Initially, I was gutted because I'd wanted the scrap, but there and then I knew that I wanted to get to know her. She was beautiful, kind and funny, and there was a connection from my direction that very night. I also knew that I was punching above my weight in more ways than just looks!

From her end, the connection was much slower, and I almost scared her off with my increasing pushiness, which didn't quite become clear until much later on in our relationship, but as an old romantic – not! – I persevered, and very soon it was clear that we were meant to be.

The ticking bomb that was me and my poor mental health, continued to tick, and even after I'd given Michelle my heart and started to let the mental titanium wall down with her, it was clear that the explosion from within was even more imminent. There was no chance of a U-turn or of any type of proverbial disposal unit arriving to detonate me safely. Year after year of mental torture was catching up with me.

'You've got to get help!' Michelle insisted after we'd been together for a few months, and after I'd had one of many, frequent paranoid outbursts.

I'd fly accusations around that had no weight behind them, except in my head. My 'norm' was completely fucked up at this stage. Life had taught me not to trust, that no matter how nice they were, people would take advantage of you in the end. It didn't seem to matter what anyone said. I'd hear them, but it didn't change how I thought. No amount of reassurance even touched the sides.

Years of practice in every other relationship I'd been in meant that I was brilliantly convincing with my arguments and was able to twist my insecurities into all shapes and sizes, depending on what outcome I wanted or needed.

It's easy to say that I wasn't doing it on purpose; I honestly didn't want to cause Michelle any hurt or stress. I was mentally ill, but I didn't recognise it or want to recognise it. Truth be told, I'd probably been mentally ill since childhood; but with no one to identify it or support me, I knew no different. I'd never had admitted to it anyway and would have been mortified by the very notion of it.

Behind the polite charm, my head was a constant, dense mass of insecurities and fear that Michelle would leave me, like I'd felt with everyone in every other relationship I'd ever had. How could I have possibly thought anything else, when I'd been told, practically from birth, that I was of little importance, devoid of any love or nurture by a family that had only existed because of an unwanted pregnancy?

Concepts in my head that should have been a natural result of nurture were missing or, worse, had linked to other concepts that made my thought patterns inaccurate in the world around me. The trouble was, I knew no different. This had been my norm for so long.

After many explosive episodes with Michelle, there was no other option. 'If you don't get help, we can't be together,' she said. 'I'll help you, but you have to be willing to change.'

Michelle was important to me and I knew she was right, so I embarked on a rollercoaster ride that began with counselling and then continued through a referral to a clinical psychologist. Quite quickly, this became serious stuff, and treatment took up not only most of my time, but practically all of my thoughts, too. As difficult as it was, I never missed an appointment. I was so determined to get to a better place, to have a life free from the demons tormenting me inside. Meanwhile, the public cover-up continued (God forbid that anyone would find out), and so did the internal crucifying shame. Looking back, I only have shades of memories of those early months and years with Michelle.

My treatment was all consuming and often meant I was repeatedly mentally traumatised by what I was uncovering from the very core of my being. Of course, normal life had to keep going, too, even with the disruption and disturbances that my treatment brought with it. My relationship with Michelle grew roots of trust and honesty – real trust and real honesty – which was something I'd never truly experienced before.

We married at the turn of the millennium, in 2000, with just over thirty people celebrating with us, Michelle's family and close friends, and my close friends. My family didn't come. In fact, I'm not even sure now if I invited my parents. If I did, it would have come with the clause, 'but don't worry if you can't make it.'

It was a relief in many ways that they didn't turn up. My loyal friends were there for me, and they were all the family I needed. Our wedding was very simple and easy going, mostly because my mental health wouldn't have coped with anything other than simplicity.

I hadn't been able to work due to my ill health, an embarrassment that I tried to make excuses for, and tell white lies about, to cover up the fact in front of everyone other than Michelle. Then, as the fog in my head started to become a little less dense, we decided that we'd be better off moving closer to Michelle's family, especially if we were to ever consider trying for a family.

Of course, we'd spoken about this in great depth and we both wanted to have a family together – another person to complete us, a little person to influence and love unconditionally. Inevitably, though, we were cautious. Sure, the fog was beginning to clear a little in my head due to the intense treatment that I was still having, but it was essentially early days and it still knocked me about. The very last thing I wanted was to bring another life into the world only to be unable to support him or her financially, mentally and emotionally.

5

The experience of past relationships had made me more guarded because I'd fucked them all up; every single one of them. I'd even had a chance to be a dad when I was much younger and completely fucked that up, too. The fault was all mine. I didn't have the capability or capacity to be a good dad or partner, so this added massively to my caution. Now I was with Michelle, I wanted my chance of being a proper dad in a proper family if I could.

We were nearly two years into our marriage before we finally decided to begin trying for a family. It gave us both something to think about that was positive, that offered a look to the future and the beginning of a new chapter.

However, weeks turned into months and there was no sign that Michelle was pregnant. She eventually visited her doctor who referred her to a fertility specialist for further tests. The appointment was months away, but we were patient, knowing that at least someone was going to assess her and investigate any reasons why she wasn't becoming pregnant. In the meantime, we didn't mind practising!

The appointment was for mid-May, so the thought of pregnancy had been essentially put on the back burner for me. I was prepared for the systematic run of appointments and tests that were forecast. Naively, it didn't occur to me for a second that the tests might reveal that we'd not be able to have children at all.

3

On Sunday, May 4th 2003, I'd been working late and came home tired, and also a bit flustered. We were due to spend the night at the home of Michelle's brother Patrick's and were also going out for dinner with him and his wife that evening, something we tried to do whenever we could arrange it. They lived a good half-hour's drive away, so time was of the essence when I arrived back home, and we had to get a move on. I showered, changed and was ready to go. Then, just as we were about to leave, Michelle arrived in the living room with a sly grin on her face. I didn't really take much heed until she pulled a decorated gold box from behind her back and presented it in front of my face as I sat on the sofa.

'Open it!' she laughed.

'What is it?' I laughed back. As a real man's man, a rectangular gold box that shone different shades of gold depending on how the light caught it was unlikely to contain a gift that I'd like, surely!

'Go on,' she said. 'It's nothing bad!'

Casually, I lifted the lid of the box. Initially, all I would see was a shedload of pink shredded crêpe paper and was none the wiser.

'Look inside it!' Michelle insisted.

Removing some of the fluff revealed a white stick with a bit of colour in the middle. Not being in the frame of mind necessary to catch on quickly, it took me about a minute to realise what it was I was looking at. The penny finally dropped, and I knew it was a pregnancy test. Surely not, no way; was Michelle telling me she was pregnant?

'Is it positive?' I screeched.

'Of course it is!' Michelle shrieked, and I was up off the settee in a flash and excitedly hugging her.

Yeah! We'd done it! Our fertility appointment was less than a fortnight away, but we'd done it on our own. Michelle was pregnant and we were going to be a family. Happy days! Amazing! The sun was shining down on us at last.

'When did you find out?' I asked, bursting with manly pride.

'This morning. I did the test first thing this morning.'

'And you've kept it to yourself all day?'

'I know! And then you said you were going to be late, and I had to keep it in for even longer!'

We both said there and then that we'd keep it to ourselves for now. After all it was really early days – Michelle thought she was about five weeks.

We were so excited, but realised we needed to head off to her brother's place, or we'd be stupidly late. The best present on the planet was about to land into our lives and we were just so overjoyed.

'I know we're not telling people, but I have to ring Michael,' I told Michelle. 'I have to, I'll never keep it in.'

Michael was my best mate from home. He's a brilliant friend – still is – and the nearest thing to family I have from home. Of course, he was absolutely delighted for us. He knew we'd been through such a hard time with my own treatment, and this was definitely going to be a new start for us.

Later that evening, me and Michelle giggled together in bed, knowing that we were holding this amazing secret between us. We were just so excited.

The weeks that followed were a mix of trying to act normally, while knowing that inside Michelle our child was growing. We were looking forward to the twelve-week scan, and the time seemed to drag. We'd talk about what we thought the baby would be like. Would it have blonde curly hair like I'd had as a child, or funny toes like me, or maybe my nose?

We'd laugh about what type of personality he or she might have. A mix of my humorous craziness and Michelle's wise logic would definitely be a force to be reckoned with. We'd teach our child to be mentally strong, nurture them with love and affection, and ground them in ways of humbleness and gratitude. I just couldn't wait. We had so much to give.

4

About six weeks later, when Michelle was now eleven weeks into the pregnancy, she arrived home from work in a bit of a state.

'I've got pains, Gary. I'm aching.'

Instant worry set in and very quickly I was imaging the worst. *Get a grip, Gary,* I told myself. *It's going to be all right.* It had to be. We deserved it to be.

Just to be safe, we booked an appointment with the doctor the following morning. Michelle was immediately referred for an emergency scan at City Hospital in Birmingham, not far from our home near Sutton Coldfield. Of course we were worried, and first and foremost we needed to know that there was a heartbeat.

When we were called in for the scan, we held hands tightly and made eye contact that said, 'I love you no matter what happens next.' Michelle was deep breathing with nerves as they put the gel on her stomach. *Please, God, please, God, let this be ok,* I prayed silently.

'There's a heartbeat!' the sonographer announced within minutes, and there on the screen I could see the tiniest human being I'd ever seen in real life. Human, yet not in any way fully formed, and immediately I knew I loved this developing baby unconditionally.

'Just give me a minute,' the sonographer said. 'I need to have a good look here.'

Oh, God, what did she mean? Michelle and me looked at each other, puzzled and a bit panicked.

'There are two heartbeats here,' said the sonographer. 'Yes, I've found two heartbeats!'

'What?' we exclaimed in unison. 'Twins?'

'Yes, twins. You're having twins!'

Jesus Christ! You could have bowled me over it was such a shock! Here we were hoping and praying that we'd even find a heartbeat, and now we were going to be parents to twins. We'd wanted a family together since we'd married, and now we were getting two children in one sitting! Life was definitely never going to be the same again.

The sonographer continued to do what sonographers do – measuring, checking, moving the scanner around Michelle's belly, while we reeled from the information we'd been given. I couldn't take my eyes off the screen. Those tiny black and white images were the first precious moments of seeing what we'd created, our future, our new reality.

The sonographer then left the room to discuss with another colleague what she'd discovered on the scan, which I thought nothing of. I presumed that, because there were now twins to consider, second opinions were the norm. Nor did I worry unduly when Michelle was automatically referred to see a consultant on the Monday that followed.

That weekend, we announced to anyone who would listen that Michelle was pregnant with twins. On the Sunday, we were at a family gathering, and friends of Michelle's brother were there with their twin boys. I remember watching those little boys running around and wondering, with excitement, what my little twins would be like.

I was bursting to get the pregnancy over and just meet them. I was so, so proud to announce their existence, and the excitement that I'd felt on that first day in the living room was back again. Michelle's sister Carol was also pregnant, with her fourth child due in the October, Patrick and his wife Caroline had had their first child, a boy, three days earlier, so the excitement around our announcement was high.

However, Michelle being Michelle, sensed that something might not be a hundred per cent right, but what did she know, really? Instinct is one thing, but sometimes you can worry and create fear when there's no reason for it. She said she just sensed something was not quite right from the medical professionals we'd met during that first scan, but I just wanted to bathe in the glow of joy that I felt. I'd been given the chance to prove that I could be an upstanding dad and I couldn't wait.

Michelle's instincts were proved right, though, and on Monday morning, when we returned to the hospital, we were hit with a hammer blow that no excited father ever wants to hear.

'One of the twins may have Down Syndrome,' said the consultant. 'We can't be sure yet, but measurements are showing that it could be a possibility.'

There was more: 'We also suspect that the twins may develop Twin to Twin Transfusion Syndrome, but again it's very early days and we'd have to monitor you very closely, Michelle, to be sure.'

Bloody hell! Of course, I knew what Down Syndrome was, but I'd never ever heard of Twin to Twin Transfusion Syndrome. We were reassured that more scans and tests were to follow and that, as this was now a more complicated pregnancy, we'd be referred further to the Fetal Medicine Department at Birmingham Women's Hospital. I didn't even realise such a unit existed, but quickly got the vibe that you weren't referred there unless things weren't going to plan.

I was slipping into a state of shock and the joyous high I'd felt just days earlier was now crushing me on the way down. We were only eleven weeks in and already we were entering a tunnel of anxiety and we had no way of knowing how long, wide or dark it was going to be. What were we going to tell everyone? How could we put into words to others that our little family was already struggling when it had only been the previous weekend that we'd told them about being pregnant and having twins?

We left the hospital in a haze of tears, shock and fear, not knowing what to do next, other than turn up the following day for tests and scans at the hospital. How could this be happening to us? To Michelle? To me?

To me… to me… The thought consumed my head. I know why it's happening to me, I reasoned. It was payback. Payback for all the wrong that I'd done in my life, payback for the revenge that I'd taken out on others, payback for the anger, violence and trouble I'd either been involved in or caused over many years. Payback for all the people I'd damaged, physically and mentally. Oh God, it was my fault. This was all going wrong because of me.

I became convinced my past was catching up with me, and that karma was biting at my heels. Inside my head, the words spun instantly, instinctively, around and around like a spinning top stuck on repeat. The *No, it isn't* thought would come to try and offer comfort, but it was quickly overwhelmed again, as I allowed the self-sabotaging thoughts to push their way past. After all, they were already well established in my head.

11

5

Everything about Birmingham Women's Hospital was totally unfamiliar to me, but as soon as I walked in, there was little other than women with big bellies. I'd never seen so many pregnant women in one place at one time. Some were outside chatting on phones, or even smoking fags; others in the lobby area were waiting for visitors, or to be collected; and the plethora of big bellies continued as we walked past the cafeteria area, following the signs to Fetal Medicine. I remember the corridor being long, and Fetal Medicine being about three-quarters of the way down on the left. We passed signs for other departments, signs where 'normal' pregnant women went for 'normal' scans, but we had to bypass them and walk on. That initial appointment at Fetal Medicine was certainly walking into the unknown.

'Take a seat and someone will be with you shortly,' the receptionist said, gently, when we finally arrived.

I was absolutely shitting myself, I was so nervous. What news were they going to give us today? Would the more sophisticated scan show that everything would be okay? Please, God, it would. I could feel Michelle's nervousness through her hand as I held it. I wondered if she could feel mine, in return. I was gripping the arm of the chair with my free hand as we sat in anticipation. We gave each other reassuring smiles, but there was no depth behind them. Both of us were scared. Both of us desperately wanted to hear good news.

Then a lady wearing what I thought was a nurse's outfit came and sat next to Michelle and introduced herself as Sandy. I instantly warmed to her. Her tone was friendly and reassuring, and she led us along another short corridor with two scanning rooms to one side and a usual hospital cubicle on the other.

We were then introduced to Professor Kilby, who was to carry out the scan. *Professor?* This must be serious, I thought – or was I just overreacting? Helen, the specialist midwife with him, supported Michelle as the scan was carried out. Again, we got to see our beautiful children on the screen, our tiny, alien-looking creatures of hope, but this time there was no sense of joy. This time we were waiting for the professor to speak, waiting on his every word.

Once completed, he asked us to wait in the parents' room at the end of the same short corridor – a very small room with just a few comfy chairs – and he said he'd look at the scan results and come and speak to us once his report had been done. At this point, my hands were sweaty and I felt I was suffocating inside as I struggled to breathe properly. Anxiety was taking hold.

I did everything in my power to hide it from Michelle and the staff that were congregating around her. Anger started to creep in and I fought with myself to keep it under wraps.

Expressing emotion had never been my thing, unless it was anger. I was an expert at that. If I was sad, instead of letting it out as sadness I'd turn it into anger. When something was beyond my control, I turned the frustration and nervousness into anger, too – and I mean real anger. There was no half-heartedness where my anger was concerned, and until it was spent it just kept coming. It was a complete release for me, but sadly not for those who got caught in the crossfire of my explosion.

I was praying in my head that Michelle and our little twins would be safe.

Please, God, let them be okay, I prayed. *Stay positive.*

Professor Kilby arrived and sat with us. The space was far too intimate for the news that he was delivering.

'The scan results show that we do indeed suspect Twin to Twin Transfusion Syndrome,' he told us. 'We'll need a few weeks of scanning to confirm it for certain, but as the babies grow it will become evident.'

He continued to detail what Twin to Twin Transfusion Syndrome (TTTS) was, but I didn't hear it, certainly not enough of it to take it in. I caught sentences that mentioned chances and statistics of them living, chances of them dying, chances of one living and one dying, and that Michelle would need to be scanned once or twice weekly to monitor their progress.

We were devastated beyond belief. It was all too much to take in, impossible. We sat there, visibly distressed, and there were silences that filled the atmosphere with fear and devastation. I have never felt so much pain. The sadness inside me was unbelievable. My heart ached so much that I thought it would stop functioning.

13

I knew the pain it was going nowhere, that it would dig deep and get worse, much worse. I could feel the tears inside, but I knew they would never drop. Conditioning from an early age had taught me that it was a weakness. I wish I could have cried. My world felt like it was coming to an end, and my heart had died for a split second. They say that life can change in the blink of an eye, and here we were in the eye of the storm.

As we sat, trying to take the professor's words in, I could see people passing by through the glass in the door, full of smiles and jovial demeanours, and all I wanted to do was stand up and scream, 'Don't you dare fucking smile! Don't you fucking dare!'

The thought quickly turned to numbness, like an out-of-body experience where my life had come to a halt, but the world around me continued to whizz. I felt trapped; the air felt too tight. I needed to get out of there to a space with only me in it, a silent space to counteract the loud chaos that was closing in on my head.

Of course, it wasn't going to be long before self-sabotage arrived again and the dark, destroying thoughts encased me. This was my punishment for being me. I just knew that it was. Why Michelle, though? Why the woman I loved who had helped me get through the darkest of places and helped me live again? Why her? There was no reason; everything mushed together in a haze of despair.

Following that appointment, the days rolled into one another. We were back and forth to the Fetal Medicine Department once a week in the early days, which quickly became twice weekly. Very soon it was confirmed for certain that our babies did indeed have TTTS, caused – it was explained to us – by a malfunctioning valve in the placenta, which allowed an increase of blood to one twin, leaving the other twin with less than was required for healthy growth.

A baby receiving insufficient blood was inevitably going to be a poorly baby, but even the twin who had an overloaded blood supply suffered as it put a tremendous strain on that tiny, growing heart. Both of our children were in grave danger of dying and there wasn't anything that I could do about it. I had to put my trust in the professionals, professionals I did not know. I also had to brace myself for every appointment we would have to endure, and the news it might bring with it.

Besides this, it was also so incredibly upsetting to see the lady I loved so much being so brave. These babies were her precious bundles of joy, too.

6

Being at the hospital so often disrupted every element of our lives. Michelle, a teacher, was instantly signed off work, but for me it wasn't that easy. Meanwhile, with each appointment came news that sometimes told us things were 'stable' – never 'good', or even 'fine' – but more often than not, because of the fluid build-up around the twins, it was a waiting game every time to see what they said. Every time my head was dominated by the underlying thought about whether their little hearts would still be beating or not. Had they survived between scans?

I didn't want Michelle to be going to appointments on her own, or even with one of her family members or a close friend, only to find out that the twins were even more seriously ill or, worse, had passed away inside her. Imagine her getting that news alone. It was unthinkable.

It just so happened that at this point in my life I had starting working part time doing building works on a young adult care home. Thankfully, the boss was extremely kind in accommodating me taking a couple of hours out when I needed to, and I think I only missed a handful of appointments over the many months in which we were back and forth.

I was also a bouncer working the doors at the weekends, so this didn't interfere with appointments either. Being a bouncer had never been on my bucket list. To me, bouncers had been there to have a scrap with, and I'd certainly had plenty with them growing up in my hometown. It earned me a little extra money, though, and it gave me the escapism that I needed away from home and the stress of Michelle's pregnancy.

The guy I worked with, Les, was a godsend. He was ten years my senior, but we got each other straight away and were a real dream team in the bouncer world, as far as I was concerned. We watched each other's backs, had the banter and were interested in many of the same things, and his chats and company really kept me going through so many difficult days and nights on the doors. Sadly, Les passed away a few years later, and I still miss him to this day.

Another way of escaping was to do self-defence. Beating the living daylights out of pads or sparring and sweating my body bone dry allowed me an outlet to release all of the pent-up anger, sadness and anxieties that would weigh me down. The guys at the British Free Fighting Academy definitely helped me to cope with feelings that I wasn't prepared to share in words.

I was also coping with my own psychotherapy sessions in the form of twice-weekly telephone conversations. Before Michelle's pregnancy, it was twice-weekly appointments 140 miles away in Grimsby (where I used to live) as this is where my treatment had started and where I'd wanted to continue it, but now I couldn't risk being away. What would happen if Michelle needed me?

I'd been having treatment for over three years at this point, but while there was definitely positive progress, the added stress of the situation with the twins, coupled with my own mental health journey, was hard to deal with. Whereas, before this business with the pregnancy, Michelle and me would talk about my treatment and how it was going, now I didn't want to share it with her. She had enough to worry about. She was carrying and growing our twins, and her stress levels were high because if it.

I'd tried as much as possible to hide from the outside world that I was having treatment for my mental health, because I couldn't bear the embarrassment, shame, judgements and stigma that came with it. Michelle had been the only one I'd spoke to about my treatment, and now I didn't even want to do that. I felt isolated and very much alone.

Michelle's pregnancy was the most important thing in my life, which meant that my own stuff had to be cast aside for a while, but it was easier said than done. My negative, self-sabotaging thoughts were getting stronger and harder to deal with, not easier. I'd even take out my anger and frustration on the psychologist who was treating me. He didn't do empathy; he was going to remain the emotionless professional that he'd always been. God damn it, Freud would have been proud of him.

Cunt, I'd think when I heard his voice.

What I wanted was for him to be sympathetic, empathetic and caring. I yearned for it. I wanted his advice and reassurance that everything was going got be ok, but it never came. I felt alone, lying awake, night after night, with a blizzard of thoughts whirling endlessly through my head, with every scenario more negative than the one before. I worried about Michelle, our twins and my ability to be a dad.

My own dad had made a right pig's ear of being a father and this worried me intensely. What if I turned out to be a dad like him? Experience of trying to be a dad before, and my actions thereafter, had already told me that if I wasn't careful it could be a possibility, but the fear of being like him also kept me on my toes. I'd try to counteract my thoughts by telling myself that everything was going to turn out ok and that we would make the perfect family after all.

My body reacted by sweating uncontrollably throughout the night, night after night. Throughout my treatment, this had always been one of the physical symptoms of my mental unwellness, but now it came with severe chest pains and shortness of breath. As hard as the days were, the nights were definitely harder.

7

By seventeen weeks, we were in some sort of unwanted routine with regards to going back and forth to the hospital at least twice a week. Each and every visit brought the same anxiety and the same worry. We'd walk the same walk – the lobby full of pregnant women, the cafeteria, the long corridor, the signs where 'normal' pregnant women went, and so on – which always led us back to the Fetal Medicine Department. We always wondered, 'What will they tell us today? Are the twins deteriorating? Are they going to tell us something new, something else?'

The relief on Michelle's face when, at each scan, their heartbeats were seen, was massive. They were still alive and growing, so there was still hope.

However, there was something new that day. The larger twin – Twin 2 – had an increased amount of amniotic fluid, which was not something that was good for a baby's growth, and could easily trigger labour if left. Michelle's womb would have to be drained of some of its fluid there and then.

The level of fluid in her womb was way over the safe limit. We'd been warned that this was a serious complication associated with TTTS, and that it would probably have to be repeated a number of times in the coming weeks and months. We had no idea how this was going to happen or what it really involved. What we did know was that we were scared, really scared.

What would happened if Michelle did go into early labour? It wasn't just early labour, it was early, early labour! There was definitely danger involved if they were putting a needle the size of a knitting needle – no exaggeration – into her womb. What if they accidently knocked into the twins and hurt them? Could they accidently kill them? God, I couldn't go there. The thoughts were unbearable, but what option did we have? If we said no, the twins wouldn't survive, which was not something I could contemplate either.

We were in a catch-22 situation. Michelle lay there and my God, did she squeeze my hand! I can take pain, but she was really squeezing. I was sitting there trying to cope with the emotional turmoil, but Michelle also had the physical pain to handle. Could she see the concern in my face as I tried to smile reassuringly across at her? I always hoped that she couldn't. This was not about me, though. I was just the dad. Less so, I was just Gary, the guy that not many cared about anyway, or so I believed. It would have crucified me even more if I'd have revealed any sign of weakness not necessarily to Michelle, but others who were in the vicinity. The lid on my emotional box may have started to loosen, but it was never going to come off, not if I had anything to do with it.

The medical team had mentioned that sedation was available if necessary, but Michelle was prepared to be fully awake throughout. And then the procedure began.

You could have cut the atmosphere with a knife in the scan room. It was both fascinating and terrifying at the same time to watch. The medical team made a small incision into Michelle's pregnant belly and inserted the longest, widest needle into the incision, puncturing the amniotic sac while scanning the twins constantly to make sure they were out of the way. All of it could be seen clearly on the screen in front of me.

I wasn't sure what to feel or where to look as there was so much going on. With every blink came a new experience and I have to say, a shot of anger seeped in, too. It wasn't nice having to watch someone hurt the one you loved, no matter the reason. My protective instinct was on high alert and I just wanted to reach out to the doctor and stop him. I had to fight my thoughts strongly and put trust in the team - not an easy thing for me. Me and trust don't make friends easily. When you haven't felt that trusting relationship with your parents from an early age, it's not easy to let others in; but what choice did I have now?

Next, the nurse drew out the biggest syringe that I'd ever seen. It was bloody huge. Another member of the team attached it to the needle and started to pull, drawing off the fluid repeatedly, filling the syringe again and again and again, which was no mean feat, I can tell you. It was exhausting work.

All the while, Michelle gripped my hand and lay as still as she possible could. She never complained, cried out or made a fuss. I knew why. This was for our little twins and we'd have done anything for them. Once enough fluid had been drained – over a litre and a half

20

to be as precise as I can be – Michelle had to be monitored overnight on a ward.

It was a strange one really. It felt strange not having Michelle at home and I worried that I wasn't with her, but I was also relieved that she was in the care of the professionals should there be any adverse effects from the drainage procedure. The underlying thought, a selfish one maybe, continued to simmer: what would happen if both my beautiful wife *and* our beautiful twins were taken from me? What would I do then?

That fear was gripping, swaddling and smothering. There's no way I was going to continue on planet earth without them. I just wouldn't be able to take it or want to let myself let the idea spiral out of control in my dark mind. I'd pray in our empty bed, 'Please God, take me, not Michelle or our little twins. Punish me in whatever way you want, but not them. God, don't take my family away!'

I'd try to pacify myself by saying that they were only negative thoughts and frustrations, and distraction would sometimes keep them at bay but often I'd scream at my thoughts: *Leave me the fuck alone! Leave me the fuck alone!*

I was so full of sorrow and anger – anger at myself for being such a selfish bastard in the circumstances, and towards God for putting me through this. Why would such a supposedly loving God put Michelle and the twins through this?

'God, it's my punishment for fuck sake, not theirs!'

Nevertheless, I prayed into the night, night after night, for God to help. He wasn't listening, though. He couldn't have been. He'd never listened to me. He'd had millions of opportunities to help me as a child when I begged him for help to take me out of the emotionally neglectful, destructive life that my parents had burdened me with, and nothing had every changed for the better. My loving grandad, Dad's dad, a great man, had always told me that if I prayed to God, that God would listen to my prayers. He hadn't. God obviously hated me as well. How could he not? It didn't matter anyway, I hated myself more.

'Don't be a bastard like me, God! Don't take my failings out on them! Don't let what I've done to fuck up my life affect them! Please!

21

I'll take anything that you can throw at me, just don't hurt them! I need them!'

I cannot tell you how many times I repeatedly prayed the same prayer. It became my silent mantra. My prayer and thoughts would keep me awake well into the night. My eyelids would be drooping heavily, but I'd force them open because I also feared sleep.

Dreams plagued me, too, waiting to bring what was my traumatic reality into my haunted slumber once I'd eventually dropped off. Real life and the land of dreams followed the same trend.

Having to deal with all this also had a huge impact on the therapy that I was still having. As far back as I could remember I'd suffered inside, day to month to year. For now, publicly, my lips stayed quiet and my trauma stayed inside. There was no way the selfish side of my human nature was going to be the priority now. I'd do what I'd always done: just get on with it. My own treatment would have to wait. Wise words that came with detrimental consequences.

The loneliness of my mental isolation would often engulf and overwhelm me. I'd always had a sense of loneliness and but this was now deeper and darker. Michelle had her family and friends around her, constantly offering their ear of support, but my family were not only far away geographically, but also a world away in terms of my relationship with them. My pals were back in my home town, some 280 miles away. That said, having them closer wouldn't have made any difference anyway as, had they asked how I was doing, I'd have only ever said: 'I'm fine; I'm all right.'

Any such answer became my default. My emotional fragility was hidden behind an often bright but fake smile. Showing and sharing emotions was weak. Long term conditioning had taught me that.

Looking back, though, I did have plenty of people around me. Michelle's family were always supportive to both of us, and I had loyal friends that were only too happy to be there for me. The problem wasn't them, it was me. All me. I just didn't have the capacity to let others in.

How could I let them in when I couldn't let myself in, so to speak? How could they see the real me, the once sensitive child who was now an adult, when I didn't want to see him myself? Perhaps people saw more than I knew. Perhaps they saw behind the smile and the

'I'm fine'. If they did, I guess that they also saw that I was a bit of a closed book and left me well alone. I tried to let people know only what I wanted to show. Otherwise, I wanted them kept at arm's length.

8

The following day after each drainage - seven in all - I would head back to the hospital to collect Michelle, and there would be another scan to check how the twins were doing. Every scan, no matter what was said or how Michelle felt, brought relief. They were alive and therefore hope sprang eternal.

Once the fluid had been drained, it was tested to check for many things, including any possible abnormalities, but also the sex of the twins. We knew that they'd either both be boys or both be girls, as they were identical, but we were asked if we wanted to find out for sure.

We were both thrilled and relieved to know through the results that neither twin had Down Syndrome. Relieved for them, for their future and for our future, too. And yes, we both wanted to know what sex they were, as we felt it would bring us all closer together as a family. We knew this pregnancy was a roller-coaster ride, to put it mildly, so getting to know the twins as soon as possible, in whatever way we could, was a real priority.

They were girls! There were two little girls in Michelle's tummy. Our little girls. My little girls. I had daughters! Wow! I instantly and instinctively turned into the protective father. Isn't that what every dad does when he hears he's having girls? We had to digest the information, which was odd really, as of course it was a fifty-fifty chance, so why the shock? But shocked we were.

We already loved and knew our little twins, and now we connected with them even more. I felt such pride. I started to believe for the first time in my life that I deserved happiness. For the first time, it was going to work out.

The dream and fantasy I'd had as far back as I could remember, from when I was a little boy, was to have my own *The Waltons* or *Little House on The Prairie* family, and it was happening. I'd led a life of self-destruction and destroyed everything that had been good in my life, including the chance to have good relationships and a family, but things were beginning to look up. Many years of hard work in therapy were coming to fruition. It had all been worth it; I was going to be a good dad at last.

It was my time to shine and make good. I was going to be a dad of beautiful twin girls. The old me who would constantly question how much I deserved to be a dad was still niggling, but I'd lived for long enough in the darkness of my head, and was now able to see slithers and rays of light finally emerging. I was going to continue to work hard to get there, and be a fantastic dad for my girls.

It was hard not to plan for the future – and theirs – in my head every time I thought of them. It brought the two of us so much joy to share with our family and friends that we were having twin girls.

As for me, I've always been a bit of joker, and enjoyed the banter, and as Michelle's belly started to expand – and it did at lightning speed with two babies in there – I couldn't help but call her all sorts of names, but the one that stuck was Tubby Bear.

If you happened to have been a fan of Noddy when you were growing up, you'd remember that Mr. Tubby Bear was one of the characters in the cartoon. He had a real deep voice, I think, and always looked so stern to my child eyes. That bit has nothing to do with Michelle; it was his tummy that reminded me of her. His tummy stuck out like an old teddy bear's would and so did Michelle's. So, Tubby Bear it was.

Before long, this had grown into Tubby Bear and the Little Bears, quite an apt naming for all three of them, I thought. They were my Bears and I loved them all. I'd try and make up songs about them, or rhymes, which often drove Michelle mad, but she couldn't help but laugh simply at my atrocious singing voice, if nothing else! To this day, she's still my Tubby Bear.

In quieter times at home, maybe when we were watching TV, I would lie with my head on Michelle's tummy and talk to the Bears. Nothing serious, sensible or philosophical, of course. It would usually go a bit like this:

'Are you listening in there?'

We'd laugh at that, then,

'Daddy good, Mummy bad!'

And I'd repeat it over and over again to her stomach.

'Daddy good, Mummy bad!'

Michelle wasn't always going to have it all her way! Thinking back to it makes me smile even now. I couldn't wait for them to be born.

With me being a proud northerner, they were definitely going to have Newcastle United black and white striped football colours on their sleepsuits that was for sure! We may be living in Aston Villa territory now, but Newcastle United was still my team.

I wanted to be their teacher – to teach them how to walk, ride a bike, kick and catch a ball. I wanted to be the one that they came to for cuddles, who'd be there on their first day at school, anticipate their fears and be able to calm them. Every dad must envisage these things. How could you not?

I knew that I wasn't going to find it easy, not by a long shot, but I was going to do my best, my very best. My own family hadn't set me much of an example, but I was determined to break that chain and be a better dad than I'd seen others be and a better man than I'd been in the past. Michelle would be my guiding light. I wasn't going to be like my past anymore, but I did worry, too. What if I did end up being like my own dad or worse? How could I be sure that I wasn't going to be? What if it was now naturally bred into me to be the same? Surely that wasn't going to be the case, and anyway, I'd worked so hard to unravel the bad examples I'd been set and previously followed.

I would show the Bears love, protect them from harm in a way that only dads can – and monitor their boyfriends, of course. God, they weren't even born and I was jumping way ahead to boyfriends! Best leave that one on the backburner for the time being, eh?

I would teach them self-defence and how to keep safe. Would I be a pushy dad? No, they would be their own people and be happy to be themselves. I'd tell them to always do their best and never give up on life, no matter what it threw at them. Michelle taught me how to be loving and I would definitely want to pass that on to them. Sure, there would be lessons in love and heartbreak along the way, but that was what life was all about and I'd let them know that, too.

Mistakes would be made, but they would only be mistakes if lessons weren't learned and forgiveness withheld. I'd tell them, 'Trust your instincts. Stand up for injustice and make the world a better place.' Kindness to all would be an important lesson. I wouldn't want them to have the somewhat selfish nature that I grew up with. On a lighter note, would they wrap me around their little fingers? Probably!

9

There was no let-up in my own therapy during all of this either. There couldn't be. I'd come a long way and needed to keep the pressure on myself to sort my own head out. Easier said than done, though. I was meant to be keeping my full attention on Michelle and the twins, surely, but if I didn't continue with my own treatment I'd be left half better.

I felt intensely guilty about this and questioned whether I really needed to see my treatment through to the end. Me and Michelle agreed that it was essential to continue, and would be more damaging to us as a family if it stopped. But of course, this new life stress was at the forefront now, and much of what I'd been working on from my past had to be shelved, at least for a while.

Meanwhile, the scans continued twice weekly, and it seemed that every visit came with negative news. Weeks began to merge a bit as there was little else to hone in on. One such week, we were told that the scan had detected possible fluid on both developing brains, and that the larger twin was working so hard her heart valve was thickening.

What were we going to do now? It was still early days and there were already so many complications. We were devastated for our Little Bears all over again. Professor Kilby was articulate and empathetic with the news and updates that we continually got, but although I listened, or rather tried to listen, the information went in one ear and out of the other.

It wasn't through a lack of concentration; I just couldn't take the information in and hold it in my head. I didn't want to process it; I didn't want to hear anything negative. I just wanted to hear that they were all going to be okay, but no one had said anything about that to us yet, so I continued to wait and simply never digested any other information. I just wanted positive news and closed myself down to the negative.

It was as we sat with Professor Kilby that gently, considerately and with great sensitivity, our midwife Helen told us, 'You know that you still have the choice whether or not to continue with the pregnancy?'

'No, we wouldn't consider that,' Michelle quickly interjected, shaking her head. 'We want them no matter what.'

I couldn't have agreed more. I'd never felt love like I had at this moment in my life – not even my past love of alcohol and that was saying something. There had been a time not too many years before that I'd have sold the coat off my back – or yours – for the love of drink, which is another story; but this love that I felt now was something way out of that league.

The Bears were my flesh a blood, a chance for me to be a good father and for me to protect them from all life threw at us as a family. While there was a chance they'd be born – and we'd become the family that I'd always craved, but often felt incapable of having – we were going to give our Little Bears the best chance to live. Live! LIVE!

By twenty-two weeks, it was decided that Michelle needed an MRI scan to assess the needs of the Bears in even more detail, particularly their developing brains. This was to be done at Birmingham Children's Hospital. Another hospital for us to attend – hospital number three.

We were so grateful for the care we were being offered. It made us feel that we weren't the only ones who were fighting for our little babies, and that many, many others were willing to give it a go for us and for them as well. We weren't on our own.

I remember that on the day of that MRI scan Michelle was extremely emotional when we were outside in the waiting area. Waiting rooms are serious stress areas. What do you do there, except wait and think? For us, thoughts were never going to be positive at that stage. Instead we had the utter fear about what they might find and what the scan would reveal. The reality of the situation was hitting really hard that day.

'I can't believe we're here,' Michelle sobbed. 'They're not even born yet and they have to have an MRI scan. It's so sad. Poor things.'

While she was away in the scan room, I sat and stared at the floor, elbows slumped on my knees, eyes fix to the ground.

'Are you okay?' a nurse enquired in passing, putting her hand on my shoulder.

'I'm fine, thank you,' I smiled, knowing that I was anything but. What else do you say to a stranger, though?

When Michelle returned to the waiting area after the scan, I remember her telling me that she'd been listening to the singer Dido in her headphones while the scan was happening. It's funny the little things that you recall after such a long time.

The results revealed what we kind of already knew. There was fluid on both their brains, which we were told could subside as they grew or could be drained once they were born. Also, the bigger twin's heart valve and artery were thickened and therefore unable to work properly.

The smaller twin was also malnourished compared to the other as she was receiving less blood, too. Bloody hell! What were we going to face next? How were we going to keep going?

There were so many times in the quiet of the night that we cried and prayed in blind panic, unable to fend off the desperate feeling that the Bears were going to die. I remember Michelle sitting on the edge of the bed in the spare room, sobbing uncontrollably, her eyes like rabbits in the headlights.

'They're going to die, aren't they? They're going to die! Oh my God, they're going to die!'

Her body shook involuntary and I could only sit with her and try, in a very simple way, to offer her my care and support; but what the bloody hell did care and support look like in this situation? It felt beyond me at times. Seeing Michelle in such a state when she was normally so controlled and together sent my own emotions into panic mode, too. What could I say? How could I reassure her really, especially as my thoughts at that moment weren't far behind hers?

With all of the evidence stacked against the Bears, how could they *not* die? They had so much going against them. What chance did they really have? We weren't in the protective glove of the hospital, sitting there on the bed together, with answers on tap and a knowledgeable ear. No, we were at home, alone, struggling to digest what was said at every appointment, struggling to deal with the reality of it all.

Nothing could have prepared us for the stress and strain that all this was putting on us. We'd look at each other, both with wide eyes of despair, and not knowing what to say or do to support the other one. As much as we were doing this together and supporting each other, deep inside we were further apart than we'd ever been.

30

The truth was, we weren't physically or mentally capable of taking on the other's pain. We were each superficially supporting the other on the surface, but flailing helplessly under the surface. Coupled with this, the whole thing sent my already vulnerable mental health into overdrive. I'd convinced myself that all this was just following my pattern of 'bad luck' that I'd carried with me all of my life. Wasn't it?

My natural default was to run away and take myself off somewhere where reality was a long way in the distance. I genuinely wanted to do that, and not just for an hour's respite or even a day. I just wanted to go as far away as I could to anywhere that would give me the space, for however long it took, to make the overwhelming feeling of pain and heartache subside.

I just couldn't afford to let my own emotions take control, though. I had to be strong for the Bears and for Michelle. They were my responsibility and I'd need to bury my own feelings and take theirs on. That was my job now. I was a husband and a dad. On the despairing days, every hour felt like a week, and although Michelle's hospital appointments were at least twice weekly now, the few days between appointments were sometimes long. Thankfully, compared to the days that were more positive and had us sitting on the edge of hope, those moments were relatively rare, and short lived.

10

For me and Michelle, normal life was put on hold. Michelle had been signed off work, and I was trying to take as much time off as possible to make sure that I could be at as many hospital appointments as possible. It could have been said that I wasn't needed at those appointments with Michelle, and I know that there were many other dads that couldn't make it with their partners as I was able to, but our situation was different, and the thought of Michelle being on her own when the news wasn't good continued to be a real fear for me.

How would she cope with having to hear bad news on her own? How would I feel hearing the bad news, knowing that I hadn't been there to support her? I needed to be there as often as I could and, looking back, for all thirty-nine scans that Michelle had, I think that there were only two or three that I didn't – couldn't – make. Michelle's family and friend stepped in when I couldn't be there and we kept in contact throughout.

As an aside, Michelle didn't have a mobile phone until she became pregnant with the twins, a situation that was rectified as a matter of urgency, because I never wanted her to be on her own and unable to contact someone if anything untoward occurred.

As it happened, none of my missed scans came with any developments regarding the twins that I didn't already know about. So, work fitted around appointments and the rest of our lives revolved around appointments, too.

Although Michelle felt well during her pregnancy – other than the usual morning sickness symptoms for the first sixteen weeks – emotionally and mentally we were both in a state, but there is an inner strength that keeps you going and functioning as best you can. We were living and breathing between appointments and functioning well to the outside world, but we continued to be on high alert from morning 'til night.

Light relief was short-lived, and thoughts were always turning to the previous appointment and what had been said, or the next one and the anticipation of what might be said then. It felt emotionally safer when it was just the two of us. We could see in each other's eyes that each knew what the other might be feeling, because they were feeling it, too, or if not right then, then at some other point in the same day, another day, another week or month. We were in this together, and we were either comforted in some way because of it or terrified for each other for the same reason. The waves and tides moved back and forth.

We were often not feeling up to doing very much. Going out, socialising, putting on a smile – it all felt like too much effort and too energy-draining. People were always kind and asked how things were, but in a room full of people, I'd end up having the same small talk with 10, 20, 30 people and sometimes more.

The conversation often went something like this:

'How are things going, Gary?'

'Oh, okay, thanks.'

Well, they aren't, but I'm not going down the road of explaining everything. You're being social and don't need me going off on a long spiel about my woes. If I do, you'll never want to ask me how I am again.

'How's Michelle?'

'She's doing fine too, thanks. She's getting on with it, too.'

Well, she'd not really fine, but if you look across the room at her now, you'd think she was. You don't need to hear her woes either.

Sometimes the conversation stopped there as we'd both look relieved at getting away with not actually having to say or listen to specific details about my situation, and we could change the subject. Sometimes, the conversation continued though.

'How are the babies doing?'

Well, shit! How was I ever honestly going to answer that? Say they're doing okay, but chances are they will become even more poorly and might die? That we live hoping that that'll never come to the fore? Who wanted to hear that while they were standing next to you holding a beer?

'They're doing okay. We're all just taking it one day at a time.'

Short pause, and I would steer the conversation the other way:

'So, how's things with you?'

Attention deflected. Relief all round again.

People were caring, sympathetic and genuinely interested. But having to think and filter what to say, or not to say for self-preservation, was exhausting. With that in mind, there were plenty of things we didn't do and gatherings we avoided to preserve our dwindling emotional energy within. It just wasn't worth it. Sometimes it probably didn't go down too well with some, but then they didn't get it and that was fine.

I needed to preserve my energy for Michelle and the Bears – and for myself, I guess.

On the flip side, naturally, there were things that we really wanted to do, but weren't able to do so for obvious reasons. We'd always gone to Ireland for our summer holiday. Michelle had family there and a lovely place to stay, but the summer of 2003 was going to be different. Hospitals had become our 'vacation', and there was no way that we could go away for any meaningful length of time, as we were never sure until we saw the next scan whether Michelle would need another drain.

To be honest, even if the doctors at the hospital told us that we could go to Ireland, we wouldn't have anyway. Some days, being nine miles away from the hospital was emotionally too far. We did manage to go to a local hotel for a weekend, just to get away, choosing it as we knew we were close enough to home if we needed to return.

Michelle's best friend was getting married in Ireland in the October, but there was no way that we would be able to go. Instead we were the house-sitters for her and her husband-to-be while they were away. The advantage was that their house was literally five minutes from Birmingham Women's Hospital, should we need to get there quickly, so, frankly, it killed two birds with one stone.

I remember vividly, sitting on the settee while house-sitting and watching Michelle's stomach contort into the strangest of shapes. It was like she was carrying aliens! Of course, by now, she was used to seeing it and feeling it every day, but it still looked really odd to me.

'That's the bigger one's arm sticking out there!' she'd laugh to me. It looked gross!

'How do you know? How do you know which one it is? How do you know it's an arm?' Surely, she was just guessing.

'I know. I just know.'
I'm betting she probably did.

11

As the weeks went on, the frequency of the drainages was becoming closer together, and the amount of liquid being drained from Michelle's womb higher in volume.

Each and every scan brought anxious anticipation followed by an intense relief when their heartbeats were found, followed by more anxiety as we wondered what the experts were going to say next. Amid all the trauma, I'd watch with both heartbreak and admiration as Michelle spoke to the Bears on the scan screen, and reached out to touch them.

'Our Bears' hearts are still beating!' she'd announce, mesmerised by their tiny images.

I often wondered what she was thinking about as she gazed. Was she imagining the type of mum she wanted to be? Was she promising them her endless love?

Michelle herself had had a difficult start in life. She was born at just twenty-nine weeks, weighing only 2lb 6oz. Of course, in the early 1970s, there wasn't the expertise or technology like we have now, but thankfully she still made it. She fought to survive, and live she did. Our Little Bears had a great role model to follow and I knew that they would be fighters, too, just like their mummy. I wanted to believe this wholeheartedly, and I did believe it wholeheartedly, almost all of the time.

The team at the Fetal Medicine Department had warned and advised Michelle that by twenty-eight weeks there was the chance that the Bears might have to be delivered, and told her to be ready, just in case. They, like us, were hoping that we'd make it to at least thirty-two weeks, giving the Bears an even better chance of survival. In preparation for this, Michelle was given steroid injections to help support the development of the girls' lungs, a crucial procedure that would serve them well.

At twenty-eight weeks, Michelle had drainage number seven, but there was a sense all around that things were getting to the point where decisions had to be made carefully regarding when exactly would be the most beneficial time for the twins to be born. You see, to benefit the smaller twin, she really needed to be born so that she could receive the right nourishment and continue to grow and thrive after being 'starved' in Michelle's womb, whereas the bigger twin had a better chance of surviving if she stayed in Michelle's belly as, although her heart was working too hard, Michelle was essentially 'carrying the can' and supporting her while she grew. It was another Catch-22 scenario.

We knew that the bigger Bear would need surgery shortly after she was born to correct the deformed heart element and that if the smaller twin did not survive in Michelle's womb the pregnancy would continue with the little twin still inside her. My God, how were we going to get our heads around that?

I didn't want to say too much, but the thought of Michelle having a dead baby inside her with the other twin, alive, floating beside the other for however long, was just too much. I knew that the medical team knew what they were doing and trusted their foresight, but I hoped and prayed that this was not something that we would have to face.

Come on, Bears! Keep going!

One day, a Thursday, with Michelle now almost twenty-nine weeks, we left home for the now familiar journey to the hospital and I just knew Michelle was different. She knew instantly that she'd need another drainage. The pressure she felt on her pregnant belly had increased in just a few days. The drainages were coming thick and fast now, and she'd asked me to put her regular overnight hospital bag in the car, but also another one, one that pregnant women bring with them when they're approaching their delivery date and have packed ready for the birth of their baby. It was just an inclination, she said, a precaution, a 'being ready'. But she knew. And she was right.

The scan that day showed that another drainage was imminent, but more than that, the blood flow of the smaller twin was deteriorating. In fact, it was beginning to flow in the wrong direction.

'I'm afraid things aren't looking too good for the smaller twin,' said Dr Somerset, the consultant, looking gravely at us both as he spoke.

We knew. We could see the scan images and the blood flow chart very clearly ourselves. So, what next? We stared at him for what must have only been for a second, but what felt like an hour. Instant

37

panic surged from a feeling of being in slow motion. A sensation of being out of my depth and things being out of my control took hold. Long gone were the past images of the Bears playing together in Michelle's womb, bashing into each other and providing us with a reason to smile and hope.

'She needs to be born today if we are going to try and keep her alive,' he went on.

Holy shit! What the fuck! Keep her alive? The on-the-spot reality of the situation was knocking – no, banging – at the door and it wasn't going to be asked to come in, it was already seeping through the gaps.

Jesus Christ! She might die, here and now, without anything happening next. My Little Bear might die on the screen while I'm standing here holding her mother's hand! Please, little one, please keep breathing or whatever it is that you have to do inside your mummy's tummy, just keep doing it, over and over and over and over again!

'You'll have to give me a minute,' Dr Somerset continued. 'I'm going to go and check our neonatal unit. Unfortunately, I think it is already full. I'll have to do some checking.'

What? Full? Does that actually happen? I'd never had to think of that before, so was amazed that it was actually a concept. So what happens now? Where would we go? Who would we go to? Or were we just going to stay and wait? Were they going to delay the Bears' need to be born until space became available? What was going on?

Dr Somerset returned with another member of the team. 'I was right,' he said. 'There are no neonatal cots available here. In any case, we'd need two cots for your twins. We'll have to ring round the local hospitals to see if they have spaces for two premature babies.'

I could tell instantly that this might be a bit of a big ask. The likelihood of two neonatal intensive care cots being available in one place? A single cot, maybe. Two cots? Slim, I was guessing.

'We're just going to call another member of the team back for the training session to come and support us, too,' he continued.

You see, on that particular day, the Fetal Medicine Department was actually officially closed. All the staff were on a training day within the hospital and Dr Somerset and Nia – the most caring and

38

compassionate nurse that you could ever ask for, it must be said – had actually interrupted their lunch break to come into the unit to scan Michelle, to look after our Bears.

I bet they had not expected that their day would have been so complicated either. They'd originally intended to scan Michelle and return to their training day. That was never going to happen now. We were led out to the waiting area within the unit and tried to take some time to filter what was going on. 'They're coming too early, Gary. It's too early,' said Michelle. Her worry was followed by tears: tears of uncertainty, tears of penetrating fear, tears of the unknown. The quietness of the empty unit only added to the stillness of our fears. All we could do was sit together, holding hands, squeezing them together like it was going to help, and wait. Wait and stare at nothing, trying to take control of the uncontrollable.

After what felt like a lifetime, Dr Somerset arrived back to us and announced that he had found a hospital with the necessary two neonatal intensive care cots.

'Shrewsbury?' we shrieked in unison. 'Shrewsbury?' we repeated, unable to believe the initial destination.

'Yes, I'm afraid so. None of the local hospitals can offer two cots and that's no use to you. The nearest place that has two cots is Shrewsbury Royal Infirmary.'

Shrewsbury was about sixty miles from where we were now sitting, and felt like a world away from what we knew. If you know in advance that you have to go sixty miles to have your baby, then you're prepared – like, for example, from my home town, it's sixty miles to the hospital in Newcastle so people *know* that that's the nearest hospital and are able to get their heads around it. But we'd expected to have the Bears here, right here in this hospital under the care of the Fetal Medicine Team, a team that we had known and trusted over so many months, a team we had confidence in. We'd never considered any other outcome.

On top of this was the urgency of the situation. Our Little Bear was fighting for her life inside Michelle, and here we were being told that we were now going to have to leave for yet another hospital, one that we had no knowledge of and where we didn't know any of the staff.

I didn't even know where the hospital was in Shrewsbury, even though I'd visited the town itself in the past.

This was the most important day of mine and my soon to be family's life, and we were going to be amongst strangers, and in a strange place at that.

12

The Fetal Medicine Team could see we were totally stressed out, and instantly knew the lack of intensive care cots at Birmingham Women's Hospital had just added to our already traumatic day. Our Little Bear was dying and we needed to get her out ASAP, but the ASAP was sixty miles away! *Shit! Shit! Shit!*

We learned quickly that it wasn't just a case of 'claiming' an ambulance from out front to whisk us off to Shrewsbury. The system worked by requesting an ambulance team from Shrewsbury to come here to collect us, and take us back to Shrewsbury. What? So, the ambulance had to travel 120 miles before we even made it to Shrewsbury Hospital? How long was that going to take? At this point we were not even sure if the request had been accepted or whether an ambulance would be available, and if so, when it was even going to leave Shrewsbury, let alone take us back with it.

Meantime, we had to ring people. We had to let close friends and family know what was happening. We'd left home a few hours ago expecting to be back there later in the afternoon, but there was no going back there today – or for many days to come, it seemed. We left the Fetal Medicine Department and went outside. The fresh air was in contrast to the stifling heat of the hospital.

Michelle wanted to ring her parents, (who were on holiday in Ireland), but rang Carol and Patrick instead. They'd get in touch with her parents. I rang her brother Paul and my mate Michael. It was such a shock for everyone. Sure, I was going to be a dad to twins very soon, but we'd spent so many weeks and months at Birmingham Women's Hospital that that's where everyone expected us to be, not in Shrewsbury. My emotions were all over the place. Michael couldn't believe that with the number of hospitals in a big city like Birmingham they couldn't accommodate us locally.

By this time, the rest of the Fetal Medicine Team were returning to the unit after their day's training, and were as shocked as we were when they saw us sitting there waiting for an ambulance to arrive. They didn't want to add to the stress of our circumstances, and were just so supportive and empathetic. They knew what we were about to face. The wait was endless and tedious. Fair play to the Fetal Medicine Team, they waited with us. They could have gone home –

they had no reason to stay, after all, and we all know what it's like when you have a training day at work. An early finish is such an added bonus, offering a chance to catch your tail, spend a bit more time with family or do something that your normal working day doesn't allow; but they stayed and supported us and joined our waiting game. I cannot even begin to express how significant and important this was to us. That professionals, the people who were now at the close of their care for us, were still willing to be there for us, right up to the very end.

We all chatted periodically while we waited, nonsense chat that passed the time. It was a relief to fill the silence, as silence equalled fear. We laughed about the fact that the team were trying to feed me chocolate and snacks from their lunches, while making sure that Michelle remained nil by mouth. She had the certainty ahead of her that later that evening she was going to have an emergency Caesarean section under general anaesthetic. I was the bystander. God only knows how she was holding it together.

After a further two hours, the chat was interrupted by the arrival of the ambulance crew from Shrewsbury. Instantly the atmosphere changed and everyone was back into medical mode and uncertain times. Nia efficiently explained in detail what needed to be said, and I remember clearly her frustration when the ambulance crew repeated more than once, 'She's not in labour though, is she?', like that was some sort of barometer for how serious things were.

Nia's patience was controlled but brewing in frustration and anger. 'No, she's not in labour, no, but Twin 1 is in a critical condition. There's a team waiting for her in Shrewsbury. You need to get her there as soon as possible.'

I have the utmost respect for all ambulance staff, but that evening the reaction of that particular crew was incredibly blasé. Maybe they were pissed off that their shift had been extended and they'd had to travel a huge distance in heavy traffic to get here, knowing that they had the same battle with the rush hour on the way back. But surely, they realised the seriousness of the situation? Whatever, they were very casual about the whole scenario. Nia was furious, which the crew were slowly becoming well aware of.

42

Most importantly, though, we had to get to Shrewsbury, and eventually the time arrived for Michelle to be put on a stretcher.

It meant our time at Fetal Medicine had come to an end, and there were lots of hugs and tears from all quarters, but few words needed to be said.

Michelle was wheeled backwards out of the department in the reverse journey to the one we'd walked only a few hours before. How quickly things change, eh? It was like one of those scenes from a film where someone is, say, at an airport and their loved ones are walking away, slowly towards the plane, emigrating to some faraway country, fading into the distance, leaving loved ones behind – that's was it was like in that moment. We were leaving, and they were watching us go. It was all utterly surreal.

Nia accompanied us to the door of the ambulance and wished us both well. Her hug was so sincere and caring, and so needed, too. Then the doors closed and we were alone with the ambulance paramedic. She checked on Michelle and then left us to it, moving to the front of the ambulance to sit alongside her colleague.

It really felt as though they thought of this job as being delivery drivers, transporting a package, but they were transporting the most important package in my world, a package that was in grave danger of being torn apart.

Michelle and me were back to holding hands again, her from the stretcher and me from the chair. We didn't chat much. In fact we were both like rabbits in the headlights, confined to the ambulance space and unable to see out. I wasn't even sure where we were most of the time and knew that the traffic situation in Birmingham during rush hour was not going to help our need for speed.

I remember our first real-time checkpoint telling me where we were was coming through the Queensway tunnel in the centre of Birmingham, heading out towards the M6 motorway. Anyone who knows this tunnel knows it's an ingenious work of engineering from half a century ago, that runs around and under the centre of the city for about half a mile or so. I knew we'd hit it as there was darkness, followed by the flashing blue lights streaming into the windows from the roof of the ambulance. I hadn't even thought about being blue-lighted. Thank God for blue lights.

As expected, the M6 was hideous. We joined at Spaghetti Junction and knew that we had another five junctions before we could leave the mayhem of the M6 for the M54, a more open motorway. Meanwhile, I could hear the paramedics chatting about this and that, but I didn't join in the conversation unless they spoke to me directly. I was just sitting there, in the realm of not knowing what I was thinking or even what I should be thinking. I wasn't even wondering what Michelle was thinking or feeling. I simply sat in the back of the ambulance keeping my thought processes at capacity. It's a good job my body breathes without me telling it to.

'The Bears are gonna come tonight,' Michelle said, looking over at me. 'They're gonna be born tonight.'

'Shit! We need to think about what to call them,' I laughed. 'We have to call them something other than the Bears.'

Of course, leading up to this point, we'd had many laughs and jokes about what we were going to call them, what and who different names reminded us of and what names we definitely weren't having, but we hadn't decided on anything. I'd been a right bugger at school and made rude rhymes up about most of the girls in my year group, so every time Michelle suggested a name that I'd known from school I'd happily recite the rhyme, much to Michelle's disgust and she'd answer, 'We're not calling them that, then!'

We'd laugh and I'd relay the story from memory about how the song came about in the first place. I'm sure you are getting a picture of how my best years were spent at school.

'So what are we going to call them then?' Michelle asked.

She began reeling off a few combinations that we'd mentioned before. We couldn't have known that naming the Bears was just round the corner so hadn't come close to any decisions before now.

'What about Alana and Dana? They fit nicely together.'

I knew instantly that they were the right names, perfectly fitting for our Bears.

'Yeah, Alana and Dana it is,' I replied, nodding and smiling. 'Alana and Dana. Alana can be the big one...'

'...and Dana the little one,' Michelle finished.

We squeezed hands and suddenly everything became even more real. Such a huge decision made, their names forever from this day

44

forward. Certainty in such uncertain times. Wow! No more labels of 'Twin 1' and 'Twin 2'. The Bears had names now, they weren't just our Bears. They were Alana and Dana Anderson.

13

I'm sure it felt like an age before we got to Shrewsbury, shortly after 7pm that evening. It was dark outside when the ambulance doors opened, and Michelle was wheeled straight into the maternity unit, where we were met by a whole team of medical people. It was evident they'd all been waiting a long time for our arrival, and were as relieved as we were that we'd arrived – us because we needed help urgently, and them because they weren't standing around playing the waiting game any longer.

It's freaky and amazing that the second we met the team, we were in their hands, trusting them like we'd known them all along. What choice did we have? We needed them and had to put our faith in their professionalism and expertise.

They needed to scan Michelle first. They needed to see what condition the journey and delay in delivery had had on Dana particularly, our little tiny Bear. We waited with bated breath to see if there were still two heartbeats and two babies moving on the screen. We knew that if Dana had died on the journey that they wouldn't deliver Alana, but would leave her inside Michelle to grow and get stronger.

Shit, I thought, *just keep going, Bears. You're nearly there.*

'There are two heartbeats,' the consultant said.

Thank God for that! They'd made it. They'd made it this far!

Within seconds, though, any shred of hope was put in jeopardy. Dana's heart rate started to slowly decrease, the numbers descending like a digital speedometer. It hit as low as forty beats per minute and lower, before quickly springing back to normal. It needed to be at least four times quicker to be anywhere near normal. No sooner had the rate re-established itself, it went crashing down again, then again, in quick succession, to seriously dangerous levels.

Dana was in real trouble. She was dying. Fuck me, get her out!

Things moved so quickly then. Before you could blink, the small scanning room was full of medical staff, all doing different jobs – consultant, anaesthetist, nurses. I tried to hold Michelle's hand and told her, 'It's going to be okay.'

But I was clearly in the way, so I stood back against the wall, just looking on as the professionals did what they knew best but what looked like complete mayhem to me. I felt useless not knowing what to do or where to go.

'You'll need a catheter, Michelle, compression stockings and a gown on, so we'll do that now,' one of the team told her. 'We'd usually catheterise you under general anaesthetic, but we'll do it here if that's ok with you as we won't have time in theatre.'

There were medical personnel preparing Michelle from head to foot. One nurse was undressing her and putting on the stockings, another poised to insert a catheter, someone else putting a cannula in, while the anaesthetist tried to read through the pre-op paper work with Michelle and get her to sign it. I'm surprised that she heard a word, or was compos mentis enough to sign it with all that was happening to her. I remember looking on in horror as the catheter was inserted at the same time as a cannula was put in her arm, but Michelle took whatever discomfort it gave her and never complained or made any fuss.

'Okay, let's go,' the anaesthetist commanded. 'Is everybody ready?'

All answered and nodded. The consultant had already left the room to scrub up. The trolley brakes were released, and Michelle and my precious Bears were wheeled out into the theatre next door.

There was a clear atmosphere of controlled urgency but my own panic was completely unleashed. I knew that this was it.

'Love you,' we mouthed to each other as they wheeled her out at a speed the emergency required.

'Phone someone, Gary. Don't be on your own!' she called back. She was still thinking about others.

And then the theatre doors closed and I was left standing, helpless and staring aimlessly. I was lost in the reality of how big this was. I paced outside the theatre doors, thumped frustration and heartache into the corridor walls with my fists, as chills struck through my body in the warmth of the hospital.

What if they all died tonight – Michelle, the Bears, my beautiful family – in that theatre, in front of me? The thoughts screamed like a banshee inside my head. If they died, my life would end tonight, too. There was no way I was gonna keep going. If their lives ended tonight, so would mine.

47

'Call someone,' she'd said. Call someone? Who was I going to phone? Most people in this situation would probably phone someone from their family. My thoughts went straight to my home town and the family that wouldn't even know that the Bears were going to be born, let alone be willing to come and support me. In any case, home was somewhere between four and five hours away, so even if I rang my mate Michael he wouldn't be able to get here. Anyway, I couldn't expect him to drop everything and come to support me.

I couldn't think straight or work out who to ring, but a noise to my left interrupted my thoughts: footsteps, fast and purposeful. I looked up and walking towards me were Michelle's brother Paul and his wife Margaret. Oh God, was I glad to see them, but the worry in all of us was quite clear.

'Call someone,' Michelle had shouted, but her shout had obviously been heard long before it'd come out of her mouth and long before I'd been able to do anything about it, as her brother and his wife had already travelled the sixty miles to Shrewsbury, and were here, now, in front of me, here to support me.

I'd phoned Paul when we were still at Birmingham Women's Hospital to tell him what was happening. He had jumped in his car from wherever he was working outside of Birmingham, drove home – probably like a fucking lunatic – picked his wife up, leaving their four young children in the care of one of Margaret's relations, fought their way through the rush hour traffic on the M6 and they were now here, standing with me.

At the time, it didn't occur to me that they were really here for me. I just presumed they were here for Michelle. They were here for her, of course, but also for me, because they knew Michelle would be out for the count in theatre for ages, and that I'd be on my own. They'd come to keep me company, make sure that I was ok and to see if there was anything that they could do. They'd come to be with a mentally, fucked-up bloke who, through conditioning, was not even able to see that they were here for him. It overwhelms me to think of their kindness. I'd really never been gladder to see anyone in my life.

'How's it going? What's happening now?' they asked frantically.

They knew that things had been a real emergency. Isn't it weird how people still try and be a bit upbeat even though the situation is so critical? That's what we were doing, or trying to do. Not only were they worried about the twins, but also about Michelle. I tried to fill them in on what had happened so far, but I'm sure my sentences were all confused and muddled. I couldn't think straight.

'She's in there now. She's all right.'

Of course we all knew that none of this was 'all right', but words failed me and I just needed to bat the reality away. The shortness of my answers and the silence that followed would have told anyone that I just didn't have the capacity to hold a proper conversation, so instead we sat, we paced, we chatted a little, we waited and we worried. We sat right next to the theatre in a small room no bigger than an alcove, not really knowing what to do next.

Without warning, the doors of the theatre opened and two members of the medical team wheeled out the tiniest human being I'd ever seen. It was one of my Bears in an incubator. They paused in front of me for what must have been only for about ten seconds. There inside, already with tubes attached, was one of my little girls. She's been born! She's made it! She's alive! I had no idea which twin it was and I didn't care. I just remember the overwhelming and overpowering sense of love that I felt.

My feelings were a mix of pure joy, and utter fear. For that split second, it was easy to put all their poorliness into the past. They were alive after all! They'd made it! Even in the first ten seconds of seeing this beautiful, tiny Bear, I couldn't believe how much I loved her, how gorgeous she was and how much she looked like me – I mean, really like me! I was definitely her dad, that was for sure!

'Wow! She's alive!'

I was in awe at what I was seeing. I just wanted to touch her, but was scared to at the same time. She looked so small and delicate.

'Bloody hell, Gary, she's the double of you!' said both Paul and Margaret together, and we laughed.

'Congratulations, mate,' Paul said and extended his hand out to shake mine, offering me the first congratulations on becoming a dad to twin girls.

Yes, she was definitely mine and I was going to treasure every minute with her. I still had no idea which twin it was but it didn't matter.

'I knew she'd make it, I just knew it!' I was completely consumed with what has just happened. Knowing that she was alive was incredible.

'We need to take her to the neonatal ward now,' said the nurse. 'You can come, too.'

Then my Little Bear was gone, pushed away in her incubator towards the Neonatal. I followed, saying my goodbyes to Paul and Margaret. We hugged, knowing that today had changed my life forever. Nothing was going to be the same, no matter what happened next.

The hug was a hug of hope: hope that the Bears were going to be okay, hope that whatever happened next would be okay, too. There was little excitement or joy in the hug and we both parted then. They walked one way and me another. They had come all that way and now had the journey home again. A long journey for such a short visit, but they didn't mind. They'd wanted to come. That's how being part of a family worked. Not mine, Michelle's. It meant the world to me.

14

I walked the short distance to the neonatal ward, following the incubator that one of the Bears was in. I know that the nurse spoke to me and her words were meant to be reassuring, but I have no recollection of anything that anyone said. My capacity to take anything in was just saturated. I looked on like it was all happening to someone else. There were so many staff all doing different jobs around such a tiny baby, I was rooted to the spot in the background.

Within what could have only been a few minutes, I'm guessing, the Neonatal doors opened and an identical incubator came towards me again. Incubator number two. My second daughter was in front of me now, slightly larger than the first, but so similar it was surreal. She was the second smallest human I'd ever seen! Both of their heads seemed way too big for their tiny bodies. Imagine that that being one of the first things I'd notice straightaway, but it was true and very evident. Of course, later I realised that all premature babies look like they've got big heads.

Now I'd seen them both I knew which twin was which. I knew the bigger twin was Alana and the smaller twin was Dana. They were my miracles and I loved them with every ounce of my being. I just couldn't stop staring and smiling in awe. I had two tiny daughters who'd made it, who were alive. Thoughts of any further difficulties were extinct. The doctors and nurses were going to look after them now. They were going to make them better and make sure they were all right.

I was totally living this very moment. I'd never felt so much love and joy in any other single moment of my life. It was total euphoria in my head. I stood there stunned, trying to take in what I was seeing. My thoughts were interrupted by another member of the medical team. It was Claire, the nurse who had been in theatre with Michelle. 'Michelle's coming round now,' she said. 'You can go and see her in Recovery.'

I allowed her to lead me by the arm in the right direction.

'She's doing okay,' Claire said. 'She asked me if the twins were alive. I told her that you'd seen them, too.'

So Michelle knew that I'd seen them. I knew this would have meant so much to her. She'd said all along that she'd been the luck

51

one to have had the Bears grow inside her for all these months, to have felt their every move and been able to say which arm or leg was poking out. All she'd wanted was for their daddy to see them, so I knew that the news would have had a huge impact. Claire talked to me the whole way to the recovery room but I do not have a clue what else she said. Her words didn't have a chance.

I heard Michelle way before I saw her. Well, at that point, I didn't know it was her, but I could hear a lady crying out in pain with long, loud, drawn-out cries of, 'Ow!' It wasn't until I turned the corner into the recovery ward that I realised it was actually Michelle. My God, could she wail!

I reached her and gave her a kiss. 'Hiya, Tubby Bear.'

'Hiya,' she croaked, not quite with it, obviously in a lot of pain and looking ashen. Once she realised it was me, all she wanted to know was about the Bears.

'They're alive, aren't they? When did you see them? Ow!'

She just kept yelling in pain. I didn't know what to do. She was trying to bend her legs up to her stomach into the foetal position to try and ease and comfort the pain of the Caesarean section.

'Don't lift your legs, Michelle,' Claire instructed. 'You'll hurt yourself even more. The anaesthetist is on his way to see if we can give you anything else for the pain.'

'Ow!' she continued. Jesus Christ!

I leant over and crouched down by her ear. 'Sh, Bear, sh. Stop screaming.'

'I can't. It hurts too much! Ow!'

This wasn't like Michelle. Her pain threshold throughout this whole thing had been incredible, so to see her in this much pain wasn't nice. In between the shouts and the anaesthetist arriving, we tried to talk briefly about the Bears, but it was still chaotic around us to say the least.

'You've seen them! When? What are they like?'

I wasn't quite sure how to answer for that split second. I was completely overwhelmed by all of it. How was I going to describe the love and worry that I felt all in one go?

'They're so tiny! They're so tiny!' was all I could get out.

Joy spread across her drowsy face, and a stream of tears falling towards her earlobes as she lay there.

'They're like me!' I added, still not sure how to comprehend what I needed to say. I couldn't help but smile and laugh at the very idea but the truth was, the Bears were incredibly like me. I wouldn't usually notice such things without being clued into them by someone else, but even I couldn't miss the strong resemblance. How could two little girls look so like me?

'They've got my eyebrows!'

I couldn't resist! This made both of us smile widely. There'd always been a standard joke about one of my eyebrows seeming to have a life of its own, so for me to have commented on the Bears' eyebrows brought a moment of light relief.

Then we sat in silence – other than Michelle's moaning – to take in what had just been said, just a few words but with so much feeling, love and emotion attached. The silent thoughts were joyful ones, joy that the Bears were alive, that Michelle had come round and that we were here together. I knew that the reality of what was happen would bite me on the arse any second and without warning, and the moment wouldn't last for long because our reality was still so critical, but for those few moments we smiled.

It must have been about half-ten or eleven o'clock by the time Michelle was brought to a side room on the ward, her pain thankfully sorted. The neonatal team, whom we were still to meet, were doing all that they could to stabilise the girls and all that we were really updated about was that they were still alive. There was no settling of any nerves or any let-up now they were born. In fact, it was abundantly clear that our time of worry had stepped up a million notches to full turbo throttle.

The last six months that we were leaving behind had felt like stress and pressure, but what was to come in the next few hours, days and weeks was going to be so much more testing seemed. The *real* worrying time was just starting.

15

We weren't allowed to see Alana and Dana at all that night. Was this a good sign? I presumed that it allowed the medical staff to do what they needed to do. Surely they'd come and get us if they needed us? Michelle needed to recover, too, and the Bears were still being stabilised all these hours later.

A makeshift put-up camp bed was put in Michelle's room so that I could spend the night alongside her, with the Bears just along the corridor. This was our first night as a family – not in any way how we would have planned it, but, most importantly, they were alive, all three of them, and I thanked God for that over and over again in my head.

By this time, it was the middle of the night. I was exhausted, but nowhere near what Michelle must have been. However, the chances of us going to sleep were slim. We were back to holding hands again, me from my makeshift camp bed and Michelle from her hospital bed. Why did we always seem to end up holding hands? For comfort, habit, unspoken words and, togetherness. We'd been through some shit together, and we were still holding hands, holding on together through thick and thin. Enough said. The room had dim lights, and the quietness of the ward let you know that no one wanted to be disturbed.

'I keep forgetting which way round the sounds of their names are,' I said in the silence, looking into space, but having spent the last half hour practising how to say Alana and Dana properly in my head. Michelle laughed. She'd been doing the same.

'It's Alana – A-LAN-A, not A-LARN-A.'

'Alana, Alana, Alana,' I recited over and over again.

'And it's Dana – D-ARN-A not D-AN-A.'

'Dana, Dana, Dana,' I kept repeating. Such similar names and spellings but different pronunciations.

'Don't put an 'r' sound in Alana, but do put the 'r' sound in Dana,' said Michelle.

'Al-A-na, DaR-na, Al-A-na, DaR-na, Al-A-na, DaR-na,' I practised, and laughed as I just kept forgetting which was which.

Silence again.

'So is it Alana or Alarna?' I'd keep piping up.

It kept us amused in the shallow light, and filled me with love every time I said their names.

'Think of Dana, the Irish singer who won Eurovision. That'll help. Then Alana is the opposite pronunciation.'

Who? It would have been helpful if I'd known who the fuck the Irish singer Dana was, or if I'd ever watched bloody Eurovision! Like I'd have ever watched that.

I lay there, thinking of Michelle, thinking of the Bears, trying to process the craziness and precious moments that the last twenty-four hours had brought. We continued to hold hands across our beds. It was all we could do.

I'd never held hands with anyone before Michelle came along. I thought it was poncy. She taught me that it wasn't and that it showed our love to each other without words. We held hands then like we'd done so many times before. I hoped that my hand in hers gave her a sense of togetherness. I know it did for me. We still hold hands all the time, today and every day.

I did managed some sleep, eventually, but it was broken sleep. Exhaustion took over and I was unaware that I'd fallen asleep. Poor Michelle wasn't; apparently my snoring repertoire was firing on all cylinders. She didn't sleep at all, not because of my snoring, but because she was on high alert, waiting to hear any news about our Bears that might be delivered during the night.

For obvious reasons, the nurses came and checked on Michelle regularly through the night. At approximately 4am, two members of the neonatal team came to talk to us about Alana and Dana. The tables had turned somewhat. Dana was pretty stable and breathing on her own with a little bit of oxygen. Remember, she'd needed to be born to survive and, although she was only 1lb 9oz she was now free from TTTS, and would hopefully gain weight and thrive. She'd had the equivalent of being malnourished in the womb compared to Alana, so her survival chances were better now than they'd been twenty-four hours before.

However, with poor Alana, it was a completely different story. She'd been relatively safe in Michelle's womb. Michelle had been her support, and although we were painfully aware that her heart was

55

working much harder than it should have been, at least Michelle had been able to help.

Now Alana had to survive on her own strength, and it was clear right from the outset that she was really struggling. She was critical but relatively stable at this point, but we were warned in the darkness about the possibility of infection, specifically necrotising enterocolitis (otherwise referred to as NEC), an infection very common in premature babies whose guts are not fully developed. It was a real and serious possibility and a danger to both girls.

Again, there were lots of words and I know that I didn't take any of them in. How could I? I was exhausted, having been pulled out of sleep in the middle of the night. Of course, the expert staff were just doing their jobs well and keeping us informed, but surely they must be aware that there is often no chance that parents will actually be able to listen and take things in.

When they'd left, me and Michelle tried to filter through the bits that we thought we'd heard. Michelle was brilliant actually. She heard much, much more than me, I've no idea how she did it, but she did. She'd try and help me process the information and answer questions that I had. She'd try to be reassuring, a role she played in our everyday life so well.

Unable to take any more, I fell back into sleep as exhaustion took hold again. I know Michelle still stayed awake all night.

16

The daylight seeping in through the blinds, and the stirring of staff around the ward, told me it was early morning. Friday had arrived. Day two with the Bears.

We were finally going to get to see them. Of course, I'd seen them as they sped past me in the neonatal ward the previous evening, but today was the going to be the real deal. I was actually going to meet them properly. I can't tell you how excited I was, but absolutely shitting myself at the same time.

I was going to meet them, but they were very sick little girls, probably wired up to every helpful contraption known to man. I was desperate to see them, but full of fear for what I might find, how I might react or how I might feel. We had to wait for a wheelchair to come to take Michelle down as she wasn't able to walk, and I could tell that she was feeling pretty much the same as me.

While we waited, I nipped out of the ward to the hospital shop that was just along the corridor. I was desperate to get my little girls a teddy. The shop had just opened and I saw, straightaway, the small, pink teddies that I wanted. It had to be two identical ones. As I walked to the counter, looking probably like I'd not slept all night (mostly true), exhausted (definitely true) and unwashed (true again), the assistant smiled at me, having almost certainly seen a hundred men in my state before. I smiled back, a true smile of joy for the purchase I was about to make.

This was my first gift to my Little Bears. I felt so proud. I'd hope they'd keep them forever, treasure them and remember that Daddy had bought them for them when they were born. To the side were cards and one said, 'It's Twin Girls' on the front with a picture of Mickey Mouse under it.

'I'll have that card as well,' I said. This was the best feeling ever. I'd write that for Michelle to thank her for giving me the Bears. Such significant items to me then and now, all these years later. I borrowed a pen from the shopkeeper and wrote the card there and then.

To Mummy,
Lots of love always,
from

Dana & Alana

These were only a few words, but they meant the world to me. This was the first card that the Bears got to send to their mummy. I was so proud. There was no holding back when I got back to Michelle's room. I presented the teddies and the card, overjoyed to have bought them. It brought light relief to the exhaustion and we smiled and chatted about the Bears having their first teddies from their dad.

Before we knew it, it was time to go, time to see the Bears. Sure, I'd been to the neonatal ward briefly last night, but I couldn't remember anything about it. I'd never been in a neonatal ward before last night. Why would I have been? It's not the type of place that's on anybody's bucket list to visit. I knew it was be a bit like a ward full of cots instead of beds. Of course it was, but not quite.

The neonatal ward was actually a corridor with four average sized rooms off it, all glass so that you could see clearly into each room. We were led to the far end to the last room. As I went in, there, on the right-hand side, were two incubators, each holding a precious bundle.

Wow! It was completely overwhelming. In fact, overwhelming doesn't even do it justice. We came to Alana's incubator first, but I was able to glance at Dana's too, beside her sister. Jesus, my first thoughts again were that they were so, so tiny. They were beautiful, innocent beings, lying still in such a chaotic and tensioned room. And they were identical. We knew obviously that they were identical all along, but when you see that identicalness in reality, it's mad! How could two little human beings be so, so alike? It was even more uncanny because Alana was double the weight of Dana, so she was a bigger version of her twin but this didn't alter any of their likeness.

'Hello, Bears. It's Mummy,' Michelle said, overwhelmed with tears, looking through the incubator's plastic walls at Alana and then being wheeled around to see Dana. I said my hellos, too, and we were able to smile to ourselves and each other.

'Oh my God, they're so like you, Gary!' said Michelle, laughing through the tears. 'Look at their eyebrows!'

She was right. I'd told her as much last night! My massive grin stretched from ear to ear. 'I wasn't lying, was I?'

Sitting staring at them now, once again there was no denying who their father was – me. How proud I felt. I wanted the world to come in and see them and shout, 'Look, these are mine! They're really mine!' The fact that they looked so much like me only cemented the sense of pride.

Everyone, from this day onwards, would comment on how much like me they were, I thought, *and every time they do I will be filled with pride.* It was such a gorgeous, but truly alien feeling.

I had the family I'd always wanted to have and was now capable of having, to keep supporting and loving, a real family – not just friends that I considered as family, or real family that didn't care much about me, or that I was unable to love in the past. The Bears were part of me, right here, right now, and the overwhelming sense of love that I felt was bursting into being. I'd never felt anything like it before.

'How can two little girls look so like their dad?' Michelle questioned, still taken aback by their likeness to me.

Still in this state of mind, the medical staff asked if we wanted to hold their hands. Their hands? Had they seen the size of them? I'd break them, surely, with my big old palms. This was really scary stuff for me, I so didn't want to damage them in anyway. They looked so incredibly fragile and defenceless. There was no rationale to the thoughts looking back, because of course I wasn't going to hurt them, but the heightened thoughts were there nevertheless.

We sanitised our hands and, in the bleeps of every pitch from various monitors, I got to touch my daughter's hand. I could only use one finger to gently stroke Alana and Dana's palms as it filled all the space.

'Hello Alana, Daddy here. Love you, Bear.'

Then I did the same at Dana's incubator.

It was all so surreal. Here I was, meeting my Little Bears properly, but all I could do was use one finger to touch their hands. One of the nurses handed us some Polaroid pictures – you know the ones that come out of the camera as soon as you've taken them and you have to shake them while they develop. A doctor had taken a photograph of each Bear soon after they were born. These were our first photos of the Bears for us to keep, and they were such special photos.

59

The Bears were here in front of us, but having pictures were so precious, too. The quality of them was poor and the focus a bit skewed, but I didn't care. I had them to take away with me. One of the doctors came in to apologise of the poor quality.

'Had I have known that those two photos were the very first ones that you were ever going to have of them, I would have taken more,' she said. 'I'm so sorry they're a bit blurry. It wasn't easy trying to take them with all of the medical staff in here.'

I was just grateful to have them. I knew they'd be so many more photos taken in the days, weeks, months, years ahead: first bath, first smiles, all the expected stages. They were all to come, but for now the very first ones were just right.

Sadly, the sadness and worry soon kicked in as I sat there. Reality kicked in. Why couldn't I just pick them up and hug them, hold them, feel them against my skin, smell them – all the things that parents normally did? There was no chance of any of that.

The fourth room along, the one we were in now, I found out later to be the Intensive Care part of the neonatal ward. Alana and Dana were critically ill and were getting 24-hour nursing care each from individual nursing staff. We sat, just staring and stroking their little hands.

Nurses were milling around us and tending to the girls, but it was clear that Alana needed more tending to than Dana, much more. Dr Deshpandi was their consultant now, and it was at this point that we met him for the first time, yet another doctor I was going to have to trust to do the very best for my girls.

He had a plain piece of paper with him and a pen. It looked a bit like scrap paper, actually, like it was the crumpled one off the printer that no one was every going to use for printing. Anyway, in a nutshell, he explained that Dana was still critical but stable, was still having breathing support with oxygen but was breathing by herself, having initially been on a ventilator. It was early days, but she was coping.

Alana wasn't. She was on a ventilator and the machine was doing the job of breathing for her to get oxygen around her tiny body. Having oxygen just from a tube while she breathed herself wasn't enough. Dr Deshpandi proceeded to draw a very basic diagram of the heart on the piece of paper, showing us how Alana's heart was working – or wasn't working, as it happened.

'She's going to need heart surgery,' he told us. 'The blood isn't flowing through properly and it's making her heart weaker. The surgery can be done and needs to be done to save her life.'

His words were delivered in a kind, and understanding manner, but were straight to the point.

'Unfortunately, she can't have it done here. The surgeons at Birmingham Children's Hospital are the experts in this field so we would have to transfer her back to Birmingham. We're trying to see if we can organise that as we speak.'

The words went in but swam around my head, making little sense. They just floated and faded. 'So, we're all going back to Birmingham?' I asked.

'No, I'm afraid not,' he replied. 'Dana will stay here and so will you,' he pointed at Michelle, 'as you are not ready to be discharged yet, either.'

'So what's going to happen?' I asked, still not grasping what was going to actually happen next, but knowing that we were going to be split up somehow.

'We're going to try and arrange for Alana to be transferred by ambulance, in an incubator, to Birmingham Children's Hospital as soon as possible, hopefully later today. We need to do it as soon as possible.'

'I'll go with her,' I blurted out, full of love and protection.

'Let's just see what happens next, for now. Things could change. Alana needs to be stable before we even attempt to move her. We'll keep you informed.'

Dr Deshpandi handed the piece of paper to Michelle and left us there, still with the bleeps and the noise and with yet another hurdle and thought process to comprehend.

The sister from the ward that had been looking after Michelle was back. 'We'll take you back to the ward now, Mum,' she said. 'You need to get some rest yourself. You can come back down later. It'll give you a chance to think about what the doctors have said.'

We didn't want to leave the Bears but you just do as you're told, as you don't know the right way or the best way or the anyway when your head is mushed up with exhaustion, fear and disbelief.

They'd moved Michelle from a side room to the family room just across the corridor while we'd been away. It wasn't as if there was a lot to move, but the room had a bed, a settee, a bathroom and a kettle. The staff were trying to make things easier for us. They knew we were miles from home and that inevitably there'd be visitors coming from afar, so moving to a more spacious room did make a difference.

Michelle's parents were there waiting for us when we got back. They'd arrived back on a plane from Belfast just hours before. When they'd heard the news that the Bears were going to be born, they'd cut their holiday short to come home to be with us.

That wasn't without its complications either, as they arrived in Belfast only to find that they'd left their passports on the other side of the country and had to make the return journey to get them. They said that they just had to come. They'd never have been able to stay away. Family was family and they were living, breathing examples of the true meaning of the word. I'd always admired them for that.

We tried to work out what to do next for the best. Did I go in the ambulance with Alana? Did I meet her there? Did I come back to see Dana and Michelle later? Daily? What would Michelle do without me? What would I do without her? What would Alana do without Michelle? Even more frightening, what would I do if it was just me and Alana? I felt so unprepared for these decisions and which way to go.

'If you go in the ambulance with Alana, your car will be left here and then you're completely stuck,' Michelle's mum stated, and we all agreed until we realised that my car wasn't even here. It was back at Birmingham Women's Hospital, of course it was. Idiot! We'd arrived here by ambulance.

'The car isn't even bloody here!' I said, exasperated yet again as the minor complication of the additional plan that had to be thought through to collect the car.

'We'll drive you there. We'll drive you wherever you want to go,' Michelle's dad stood up, ready to do whatever was needed.

Meanwhile, unbeknown to any of us at that point, Michelle's brother, Patrick and his wife, Caroline had already taken matters into their own hands and kindly gone to Birmingham Women's Hospital to try and get the car back. Bless them, they were trying to save me a job. Can you believe it, though? Whoever had 'safely' hidden the keys wasn't around when they got to the Fetal Medicine Department, and no amount of searching from the other staff members could put their hands on them. Patrick and Caroline had to leave there empty handed and frustrated! 'What happens if we get stuck in traffic? What happens if we get stuck somewhere collecting the car and miss Alana arriving?' I panicked.

'Listen, Gary.' Michelle touched my arm. 'Just do what you can. If you get near to Birmingham and it's pretty clear that going over to the other side of the city to get the car is pushing it, then leave the car. We can sort that tomorrow. I'm sure someone else'll go for it if we need them to.'

Everyone nodded and started to move.

'I'll be here for her this end until she leaves, and you can meet her at the Children's Hospital back home. The medical staff will be monitoring her all the way there, she'll be okay,' Michelle tried to reassure me.

'I'll do that then,' I said, feeling that the responsibility of being a dad was now punching me full force in the face. 'We'll just have to wait and see what the doctors say now.'

Just before I left, I wanted Michelle to leave a note from me, a message that she could hold on to in my absence. From somewhere, I have no clue where, I found an old, used white envelope. It was the nearest and only thing I could find at the time that resembled something that I could write on and likewise a random pen to write with. Thinking back, I probably got it from the nurses' station on Michelle's ward but I don't remember asking for it.

I wrote:

Love you, Shelly & Dana
Don't worry
You look after your end
Love you both with all my heart
G xxx Al xxx

We still have that envelope. The initial 'G' was for me and 'Al' was for Alana. I left it on her pillow, gutted to be leaving them behind. Alana was going to be in my care now. I was her daddy and that's was my job. Then I took a photograph of Alana to put in Dana's incubator, and a photograph of Dana for Alana's incubator, still together in spirit.

17

Michelle wanted the Bears to be baptised before Alana left; not a christening at a church, but baptised as soon as possible, right there, in their incubators. Her faith was strong and she knew that if anything happened to them that she wanted them to have been baptised, so it was something she wanted to happen straight away. Sure, I prayed to God because my grandad had taught me to, but there was little more to my faith than that.

I understood her reasoning up to a point, but it wasn't something that was important to me. I just wanted them to live and I definitely wasn't thinking about them dying. That very thought was just too much to bear so I didn't go there. Call it burying my head in the sand if you want, but there was no way I was going to think about them dying when we'd just had them and we'd come this far. They were living, not dying. They were fighters, just like their mummy and daddy.

Anyway, as it turned out, the hospital chaplain, Father Paul, was able to come at 5pm to baptise Alana and Dana. He had popped in to see us as part of his rounds earlier in the day. He was a young, fairly newly ordained priest, and I must say, as I have very little regard for priests, I almost liked him pretty much straight away, which was unusual for me, as I didn't think much of the Catholic church or its clergy at that time.

Maybe it was the fact that he wasn't the stereotypical 70-year-old, judgemental moaner who couldn't possibly have a clue about my life or anyone else's life. Me and the Catholic Church had had a few run-ins, so I was very sceptical. To me, church should be a place for the wounded, not a place where the wounded get judged and looked down on.

Trust was an issue for me already, so having an unknown 'holy man' around me who might preach that God would be there for me if things went wrong – which of course they weren't going to, were they! – was going to wind me up a treat. I knew Michelle would know exactly what I was thinking inside my head as soon as he started to speak, and that I wasn't gonna be reverent for reverence's sake. After all, he might be a complete arsehole. Most of them were. He needed to show me more than just his priestly presence, which I'm sure might have worked on some people. Otherwise I'd not be spending any time in his presence.

'So how long have you been a priest then?' I asked, wanting to judge and pull apart his every answer.

He hadn't been in Shrewsbury that long and his accent gave away that he was a Liverpudlian. This helped really, as we were able to banter a bit about the Liverpool and Newcastle United football teams. I was started to warm to him a little. Just a little. The chit-chat continued for a bit longer.

'So, what did you do before you became a priest?'

I could tell he was about my age - mid thirties - so he couldn't have been training to be a priest for more than a decade, surely. He went on to fill in the gaps. This made him appear more human and more normal. Then, no doubt to give himself a bit of street cred, he casually revealed that before he became a priest he'd had various jobs and been a bit of a lad in relationships, and so on. Well, this was more interesting now. Was he more of a bloke like me after all?

'So, have you had sex then?' I asked.

Of course, I'd gathered that he probably had from the conversation, but I had to check. I could see Michelle smirking, trying to hide a laugh and her shock, all at the same time. To be fair to the priest, he answered me bluntly, obviously realising that he was on the back foot where I was concerned.

As soon as he said, 'Yes,' with a whole load of blurb to follow, I knew he was going to be all right. He was just a bloke who at least had some experience of a life before celibacy. Of course, I had to ask him whether he missed being with women. Well, I bet you want to know as well!

Actually, he said: 'If I can train in Rome for years and resist Italian women, I'll be all right!'

I visually relaxed after that and a new respect began to arise. I'd been wrong about him and I told him as much. He was a top man. He'd been honest with me, and I returned the favour. He listened to what I had to say, and me to him, likewise.

Father Paul was able to come in at 5pm and baptise Alana and Dana. The hospital was really accommodating, even though I'm sure they wouldn't have wanted to be, really, because of having to get

Alana away as soon as possible. But Dr Deshpandi said that they would be transferring Alana pretty much straight after that, he thought.

This was a sound decision, but one that left more dilemmas. Would I go ahead, ready to meet Alana at Birmingham's Children's Hospital as initially planned? Would I miss my daughters' christening? Dads don't usually miss their children's christening, but we also knew that Alana would be blue-lighted all the way to Birmingham and there was no way that we'd be able to keep up or catch up, let alone make it to be with her in Birmingham if I did stay. Parking alone at the Children's Hospital was a nightmare and an added delay in itself.

Shit! Stay and be with my family? Go and miss the Bears being christened? Shit! No, I'd definitely go ahead of Alana and be there when she arrived in the ambulance. I didn't want her to be alone. I wanted her to know that her daddy was there, waiting for her.

So the Bears were christened there and then on that day, one day old, Dana Fiona Anderson and Alana May Anderson, but without their daddy there. I was heartbroken not to be, and jealous, too. Michelle told me it was very short but a hugely emotional moment, and she couldn't help but break down and sob. There was no one else there to see it or witness it, just Michelle and the priest amongst the beeps. She held their tiny hands as the prayers were said and the holy water dabbed on their delicate heads.

I had no intention of missing out on any other part of their lives. Ever.

18

Michelle's dad Pat drove as fast as he could. Thank God he was a good driver. There were few words in the car. I was deep in thought, thinking about everything that had happened, but I didn't dare consider what was to happen next.

The power of what had happened in just over twenty-four hours shoved any thoughts of near future to the back seat of my brain. Being here in this very moment was hard enough. I wondered about how my family were. My family, all three of them. My family. Shit, man. I just wanted them all to be all right.

I wondered about what the christening would be like without me there. I wondered, did they cry like they would have if we'd have had a normal christening in a church? I smiled to myself as I thought about Michelle. She'd definitely be crying. I was so glad that she was there with them. It ached like mad inside to know that I wasn't, but the bigger picture was just that: big. Michelle's dad, a big lump of a man with a great, big heart kept quiet, too. I knew he'd be struggling with his own thoughts. After all, I knew he loved Michelle and hated to see her going through such pain and agony as much as I did, let alone the fears that came with his new granddaughters. We were both helpless though, doing what we could in a situation that others were controlling – the professionals and God.

I kept repeating to myself, *We're gonna win this fight, Alana May. We're gonna win!*

'Oh bollocks!' Michelle's dad shouted and I was brought back to where we were on our journey.

We were about to hit Birmingham City Centre when a flash from the yellow speed camera told us that Pat was also going to be hit with a speeding ticket and points on his licence. He looked at me and I looked at him and we both knew that it didn't matter. We had much bigger fish to fry and going over the speed limit a little seemed insignificant compared to what we were all going through.

Michelle's text arrived, as planned, to say that Alana had left Shrewsbury. The pain of having to speak to each other was probably too much to bear at that moment. It broke my heart because I knew that being apart from Alana was the last thing that Michelle wanted and that she'd be desperately upset at the other end.

Collecting my car from the staff car park of the Birmingham Women's Hospital was eerie. It was there, all alone. I felt the same. My keys were somewhere inside and I tried to find someone who might be able to tell me where exactly. Maybe someone had told me before, but there was no recall of any information about them. I can't even recall who gave my keys to me. Isn't that awful? My head was so screwed.

However, autopilot kicked in and I made my way as fast as I could to Birmingham Children's Hospital, first having to argue with the security guard to let me out of the car park! For fuck's sake, why is it that when people are in crisis, others are so bloody demanding and official? It was actually another member of staff that was the 'reasoning' in the conversation. I've no doubt my driving skills were probably not top notch, but when the barrier lifted I shot out, my only concern being Alana Bear and making sure that she didn't feel as lonely as I did.

I arrived with only a few minutes to spare. Waiting was frightening. Waiting was the unknown.

I screamed to myself as the ambulance reversed into a parking space at the front of the hospital: *Come on, just open the fucking doors, man!*

I didn't even know for sure that it was definitely the right ambulance door, but the hospital staff in the ICU were ready and waiting for Alana to arrive, so I was hopeful that it was. It was dark by now, but the lights of the hospital streetlamps lit up the rear of the ambulance as it backed in.

Open the fucking doors! I repeated in my head, desperate to see Alana again, to see how she was and to see what the doctors were going to say. Part of me was also desperate to keep them shut. What if they opened the doors and told me that she'd died on the way, that she hadn't been able to sustain the trauma of the journey and had died without her family around her? I was shitting it with fear. Either way, the doors were about to open and I was gonna find out. 'Is she okay? Is she okay?' I said frantically, knowing it was Alana because when the doors opened, I could see the incubator inside.

'She's done okay,' came the response from the ambulance man. A moment of relief flooding through me: 'Thank God for that.'

Instantly, the medical team rushed to support her getting from the ambulance to the hospital, but although they were clearly in a hurry they were calm and collected, the complete opposite of me. The world was moving outside of my body, but I felt completely detached from it like I'd been put on slow motion.

I went with them because I knew that I should and needed to, but it was like I was on autopilot. My feet just did what they needed to do without my brain connecting. I was starting to detach myself from it all, with my body and mind trying to protect themselves from the trauma that the events of the last twenty-four hours had brought, like it had had to do so many times before.

I was led to a side room just outside the ICU. They obviously had to deal with Alana, not me. I remember there being another set of parents in there – a man and a woman – and trying to make stilted but polite conversation with them while we were all in such a state, each having a child in Intensive Care. I was not the easiest feeling to have to share a room with strangers. Their son had fallen out of a tree and bashed his head. He was six years old. I could tell how worried and upset they were. The mom seemed completely distraught and I guessed that the father felt as helpless as I did.

Before long, one of the ICU consultants came and asked if he could have a word with me, another new doctor, another new and unknown face that I was relying on to keep my precious Alana Bear alive. He laid it on the line, without any frills. She was very poorly – using his technical vocab – but was critically stable for now. He went on to try and explain who all the staff members were who would be around Alana's cot and how she'd get round-the-clock care, but he needn't have bothered. By then, I'd stopped listening and stopped wanting to hear. It was all too much. I couldn't take it in let alone process any of it.

'You can come in now and see her, but only for a short time.'

I heard that. As I walked, I met Dr Deshpandi, the doctor who had come to Birmingham in the ambulance with Alana. What a lovely human being he was. I couldn't thank him enough. I shook his hand with such gratefulness and sincerity. He told me that they'd do everything possible for her here. He couldn't tell me that she was going to be ok, but he didn't say that she wasn't going to be either, so

I knew there was still plenty of hope. He said that he was on his way back to Shrewsbury and that he'd call in to see Michelle when he got there. He did.

19

The Intensive Care Unit at Birmingham Children's Hospital is massive. It's overwhelming.

I have no idea whether all ICUs are the same, but this one was way bigger than I'd ever had imagined, if I'd given myself a chance to imagine it. I just hadn't expected it to be like this. For such a huge space though, it was strangely calm. Medics were getting on with their jobs and I could make out the now familiar sound of the beeps from the monitors and machines, but the calmness hit me first and foremost.

Maybe it was the contrast between the chaos in my head and the calmness of my surroundings that hit me most. Maybe it was my brain playing tricks on me. Even talking about calmness doesn't really sit right with me. After all, how could anything be truly calm in ICU? It's full of critically ill children. It did, though, have a real sense of calm, and I held that moment until it was lost again in the busyness of my mind.

I was led round to where Alana's cot was – yes, a cot, not an enclosed incubator. There she was, lying on what looked like a large pillow of softness that she appeared so tiny on top of. She looked lost and so, so vulnerable. Seeing all the medical equipment around her, the tubes, the bleeping, the displays made me feel like I was gonna be sick. It all felt so wrong. Surely God would let me change places with her.

Someone gave me a chair and I obediently sat on it. I couldn't take my eyes off Alana. Her bare chest rising and falling, every breath determined to join to the next one, and the next one, and the next one. I was fixated. Every breath one step closer to her getting better, I thought. I was willing her to keep breathing, I was there with her, watching every breath as it happened. I believed, with every bone in my body that she was going to make it, that she'd be in Intensive Care for as long as she needed to be. Then, at some stage when she was well again, we'd get to take her home.

I so wanted Alana to be the child that made it out of ICU, but for now I was her guard and guardian. It was my duty, my responsibility. I sat there, eyes glued to the cot, wondering what might come next, what the medics might say or do.

That said, I was scared inside. I'm not usually a person who allows himself to be scared, but sitting there I was as scared as I could ever remember being. Alana looked lost and I looked lost, too. She was extremely vulnerable and so was I.

It took all of my strength to snap myself out of thoughts of what might be ahead of me were Alana to get worse, but allowing the negative to take hold and grip hard needed to be a no-no. She was gonna make it and I would do everything I could to make sure that she did.

I started to talk to her, just quietly. I talked to her about Newcastle United, my friends back home and how I couldn't wait for them to meet her. I was missing her mum, so I bet that she was, too. I told her about the lovely mummy that was waiting for her in Shrewsbury and how blessed she was to have her, and that her sister was hanging in there, too. I wondered if she missed being with Dana; after all they'd spent months swimming around together in Michelle's belly. For now, though, they were apart and the only physical reminder that they were twin sisters was the photograph of Dana now placed above Alana's cot. One sister was watching over another.

A hand squeezed my shoulder. 'Dad, it's time for you to get some rest now,' the doctor said. 'Alana's stable. You need to go home, get some sleep, get some food and a change of clothing.'

I just wanted to stay. I just wanted to spend every waking moment with Alana. How could I leave her? It was night time and she'd need me. The staff, so professional and experienced, pretty much insisted that I go home and rest. I was on high alert, but they were able to see the wreck that stood in front of them. A man, a dad, totally exhausted from forty-plus hours on the most intense emotional roller-coaster. Two newly born daughters, both in Intensive Care Units but sixty miles apart, one with Mummy and one with Daddy.

This wasn't the way it was meant to be. We should have been together, all four of us, happy, healthy and enjoying becoming a family, but this was the complete opposite. This was emotional hell. I knew that Alana was still critical, but she'd stabilised, which was good news to my ears following her long journey. Her oxygen saturation rates were coming nearer to what they should have been.

Knowing this and doing as I was told, I walked out of the front of the hospital, completely dazed.

At some point I know I rang Michelle. We were both trying to hold it together at two ends in two different hospitals. Dana was stable, too, and doing well with just a bit of oxygen to support the amount of energy she was using up to breathe and I was grateful for that. I didn't know what I'd do if she was really ill, too. It didn't bear thinking about.

20

I remember sitting in my car, feeling its familiarity, but just sitting there looking out at the concrete wall of the car park that was in front of me.

Come on, Alana. You can do it!

I couldn't force myself to turn on the ignition so I just hunkered down into my seat and tried to rest. I couldn't drive home. Home seemed too far away, even though it wasn't even half a dozen miles away. I didn't want to leave her. I'd rest for a bit here and see what happened next.

I must have dropped off, but it was still pitch black when I opened my eyes again. It had only been an hour or so since I'd got into the car. This was no good. I had to go back in, my gut feeling and need to be with Alana was too strong, so I headed back to the ICU. I knew that they wouldn't let me in to be with Alana, but there were chairs outside and a small family room with more chairs that I was able to sit on. I was to spend many more hours sitting on those plastic chairs. Whenever they were doing something with Alana and I was asked to leave for a bit, my arse went and sat on them again.

I sat on the plastic row of seats right outside the ICU, then tried to lie. It was so bloody uncomfortable, but I didn't care. I wasn't going anywhere. Just being so close to Alana helped to ease the ache of anxiety that kept repeatedly screeching through my body. Around and about 4am the nursing staff came to see me again.

'Go home, Gary,' one of them ordered me. 'You'll be no good to Alana or yourself if you don't rest. It's going to be a long haul and you're going to need your strength in the days and weeks to come. Should anything change, we'll ring you straight away. Go home!'

I knew she was right. The reassurance that they would ring me if there was any change tipped the balance and I gave in to their demands, too tired to argue my case anymore. I asked if I could go back in and say goodnight to Alana, which I did. She looked so small and fragile. I picked Dana's picture up that was still looking over her sister and kissed her goodnight, too.

Autopilot drove me home. I can't recall any of the journey, so it was probably a good job it was the early hours and there weren't many cars on the road. Home, the quietest place on earth, empty of life other than mine. Home, usually a place of comfort and retreat, relaxation and celebration, but tonight it may as well have been a ruin. It offered me nothing and all I did was sit, wide-eyed, and pray.

Please, please, please God, save my little girls! Please God!

Tears rose in my eyes and blocked my throat, but I forced them away, letting anger take over. I punched the wall to let the hurt out, going from pleading with God to hating Him at the same time.

'If you're doing this to punish me, God, then give me all you've got, you bastard! You hear me, you bastard?' I'd scream to the air. 'Do what you want to me, I deserve it! I do! Just save my little girls, save my Little Bears.'

Before I knew it, night became the next day and dawn was about to break and again, exhaustion took over and I slept.

Nothing about me had changed when I woke again. I was still as high as a kite with anxiety and underlying fear about everything that was going on not just about Alana, but Michelle and Dana, too. I couldn't face breakfast, but I did wash.

Being in the house alone in all its emptiness just let my mind go bananas, so I knew I had to get out. I needed to be back at the Children's Hospital with Alana. That was where I was needed and needed to be.

I decided to get a taxi in as I had no idea when I'd be coming home again, and parking in the centre of Birmingham is not the easiest or cheapest. On the drive in, I asked to stop at one of our local shops to pick up a high-energy drink. There I saw a pink cuddly toy type thing and I whipped it up and paid for it. This was for Alana.

I'd already bought her her first teddy yesterday, but this would be her second. It cheered me to be able to give it to her and that she could keep it forever. I was her very proud dad and I'd buy her a teddy everyday if she wanted me to.

I didn't know what I was gonna be facing when I walked in to the ICU. My heart was pounding out of my chest, my eyes were popping out of my head, frantically looking into people's faces on my way in, trying to read for any signs of how Alana was doing and whether she was ok. I'm not sure what I was expecting to see in people's eyes. Hope, maybe? I was desperate for something to ease the anxiety. I had to trust in the strangers looking after Alana and that they would have phoned me if they'd been anything change. Surely they would.

When I go to where Alana was, the nurse – coincidently called Michelle, too – was attending to Alana. Another colleague came and went, too – another lovely nurse whose name escapes me now. They were both such dedicated, calming ladies, doing their job without, I'm guessing, much thought as to how crucial they were to me. Maybe they did, it's not as if I was the first, or going to be the last parent they'd be caring for.

Watching them gave me the hope that I was looking for. It didn't come from their eyes, it came from the way that they conducted themselves around Alana and I could see that they were genuinely caring for her. Neither left her side unless it was to fetch equipment or go on a break, and then the other would take over from where the first had left off.

Nurse Michelle told me that there was no change with Alana. They would still have to get her stable before the possibility of the heart surgery that she so desperately needed could even be contemplated.

I listened to the 'no change' bit. Was that a positive? Was it a negative? I decided that it was good. Anyway, we had time for Alana to become more stable. We weren't going anywhere. I was here for the duration now. I knew they'd make me go home again at some point but it wasn't going to be for another possible 18 hours or so, so I settled in, watching Alana like a hawk.

It was while I was sitting there that I pulled out the toy that I'd bought. I'd almost forgotten about it, actually. My lips smiled as I took it out of the bag, wanting to give it to Alana so that it could rest on the edge of her cot.

'Look what I bought for Alana this morning,' I said, proudly holding it up in the air for Nurse Michelle to see.

She looked and spontaneously began to howl laughing. I laughed, too, but only because I didn't know what was going on or why she'd laughed so much.

'What?' I looked between her and the cuddly toy, still confused.

'You can't put that in Alana's cot! If she looked up, it would terrify her!' and she laughed and laughed even more. 'Where on earth did you buy something like that from?'

'I got it this morning in the shop down the road from where we live. It was the only thing there to buy. It's pink!' I said, trying to justify my choice. It was then that I looked closely at what I'd bought. 'Oh my God, you're right. What the fuck have I bought? It's scary!' I even managed to laugh at myself.

You've have expected a loving dad to have maybe bought his precious little girl a delicate, powder pink teddy, or even a doll fit for a new-born baby, maybe with a flowery dress, pretty hair – you get the gist.

Well, no, this teddy/doll looked nothing like that. It had orange spiky, coarse hair, a bare chest and tartan shorts. That was it. Nothing else. Yes, its fluffy skin was pink, just, but that was the only redeeming feature. It resembled a butch, Highland log-thrower, no exaggeration! It would have served itself better to be on some sort of souvenir reject stall at the Highland Games, honestly, and even then, I'm pretty sure it wouldn't sell!

Me and Nurse Michelle laughed and laughed at how ugly it was!

Nevertheless, the edge of Alana's cot is where it sat! It was hers now, and the story behind it would always make me and her laugh in the future. Having Nurse Michelle around to talk to and have a bit of banter with gave me glimpses of light out of the darkness of the situation. Her light humour and easy-going appearance and way, was comforting.

21

Michelle's family knew how to be family.

Some of them came to see me and gave me support and some of them went out to Michelle in Shrewsbury to support her. All of them had enough on their own plates already; they all had young families.

Alana and Dana were niece's number ten and eleven on Michelle's side, and yet everyone rallied round and did what they could to support us both. It was kindness that went with what they knew families did in times of crisis. They brought food, drinks, sweets, company, laughter, hugs, concern, understanding and of course the football results.

They'd happily sit with me when I wanted, not sit with me when I wanted, take a walk with me, chat with me, pick my car up, collect me – whatever was needed to make my life easier. I was so grateful. Michelle's mum and dad had rushed back on the first plane from Ireland when they heard that the Bears were on the way. They all just wanted to be there for us. I hoped that one day I could repay the favour.

Michelle's brother Paul was with me the most. He'd been in Shrewsbury with me when the Bears were born and now he was back and forth to the Children's Hospital, too, staying all day with me on the Saturday. He was a father of four himself, and understood how it felt to be so worried over a child. I remember Patrick and Caroline coming in to the hospital, too, their own child only three months old. They were always laden with goodies for me; they knew I just couldn't resist sweets.

I truly hadn't really eaten anything since Thursday morning, so when they got me a baked potato from the takeaway shop across from the hospital, I devoured it. Apparently, I ate Patrick's, too! It wasn't until I'd started eating that I realised how hungry I was.

As strange as it seems, I felt like a bit of a pest sitting next to Alana all the time, like I was getting in the doctor and nurses' way, but they never made me feel like that. Spending all of that time, hour after hour, sitting with Alana must have surely been a bit of a nuisance to the staff, I imagine. They got little respite just to do their work without the glaring eyes of parents looking over their shoulder constantly, but they never complained or showed that I was a pain in the neck. They'd ask me to leave when they needed to, but that was all.

On one of my trips out to the plastic chairs, sitting with Patrick while the medical team attended to Alana, I met the dad of the boy who had fallen out of the tree. He looked different – the relief on his face unmistakable. His son had made big improvements over night, and was going to be able to leave the ICU that day. He was well on the mend.

'Ah, man, that's great news!' I said and shook his hand. 'Hope everything keeps going well. Good luck!'

I really was honestly glad for him. What it must have felt like to know that your child was on the mend and allowed out of ICU, eh? I hoped that one day my face would look as relieved as his, and that Alana would be allowed out of ICU because she was getting better.

When I wasn't sitting waiting on the plastic chairs, I would sometimes try to take a walk, just to stretch my legs while I waited. The hospital has this little chapel which I came across. I'm not a church-goer myself, but I wandered in to see what it was like: really old was my first impression, but really calming and quiet, too. It looked like it had been there for hundreds of years, but it surely couldn't have been if the building itself wasn't? You'd probably fit a hundred people in it on a good day.

Would God listen to me if I spoke to him here? Would he hear the urgency of my words and protect Michelle and the Bears? I sat down in one of the pews and prayed.

God, forget about me. I don't matter, but please look after Michelle, Alana and Dana. They need to be well. Do whatever you want to me, but please make them be ok.

I could feel the pain, hurt and anger building up inside me, bubbling, fighting to make its way out. I was frightened of my own emotions. I didn't know what to do with them or how they'd come out, so I left before they had the chance. I couldn't stay in the chapel any longer. It made everything too raw. Somehow, I ended up in the basement of the hospital – fuck knows how – I must have pressed the wrong number on the lift or something.

Where the fuck was my head at? Everywhere and nowhere. I walked out of the lift to what looked like a staff canteen area. It

80

definitely wasn't for people like me, I could tell, even though it was empty. It was eerily quiet considering all of the busy commotion that was going on in other parts of the hospital. There was a vending machine lit up in my view, so I got myself a can of coke and a bag of crisps and headed back in the direction I was meant to be in the first place, back to Alana.

At some point in the early evening – it must have been about 8pm – me and Patrick were sitting with Alana. At that time, the ICU had Polaroid cameras, too, like the ones in the neonatal ward in Shrewsbury. Patrick picked up the camera, went to one side of Alana's cot and I crouched down on the other side so that my head was in line with Alana herself. Snap. The instant photo was taken.

'That's a good one,' we agreed.

Me and Alana together. My face was literally a picture. Pride burst from the pores of my skin and shone through my eyes, and my massive smile filled so much of the photo. She was my little girl and I was her dad. The first picture of me and Alana together and would be the first to go into her baby book, I'd make sure of that. I smiled as I looked at the developed photo. Me and Alana – a picture I'll treasure forever. I put it alongside the photo of Dana, still at the side of Alana's cot.

Shortly afterwards, I could tell there were more medical staff popping back and forth to Alana's cot. They were watching the monitors and talking about her oxygen saturation levels. They were starting to slip. I could feel the tension growing a little and again tried to check out the expressions on people's faces to see what I could glean. It wasn't long before a doctor came and spoke to me.

'Alana's oxygen saturations are lower than we'd like them to be,' he told me. 'Even with the ventilator that she's on, there's not enough oxygen pumping around her body.'

'So what does that mean? What can you do about it?' I asked.

'Well, we do have the option of putting her on a different type of ventilator. It will hopefully open up her lungs even more, allowing more oxygen to get in. It's different, because it vibrates through her lungs to expand them.'

'And how long will she be on that one then?'

'We've no way of knowing yet. We'll just have to wait and see how she responds to being ventilated differently. She's still very poorly, but we hope that this will help with her saturations.'

Again, I was left without really knowing what it meant but knowing that I'd heard that it would help her. I agreed with what they were saying. Anything to help her out. Anything to make her feel a bit better. So I returned to the plastic chairs while all that was happening. They'd told me that they'd carry out the new ventilation, get her settled and then I could come back in.

Another day was coming to an end and I knew that it was late into the evening, but sitting waiting always dragged, even when I had company. Paul was still with me and to be fair the banter did keep us both going, but waiting still dragged. I guess it was the sense of anticipation that came with waiting that I wanted to be over rather than the waiting itself.

I just wanted to be in with Alana, but when I returned the sight was a bit shocking, to say the least. The nurse had warned me to be prepared and explained what I was going to see now that Alana's ventilator had been changed – but words never really prepare you for anything, do they?

Oh, how different things were now; how different someone can look in a matter of minutes. Her tiny, fragile body was literally vibrating from head to toe. Her little chest was bouncing – not in a vicious or cruel way, just evenly vibrating – like your cup of tea would if someone had a jackhammer drill outside your house. I know that's not the best comparison, but it kind of rippled over her whole body. Her eyes were duller and her body still limp.

My heart and soul were bursting with sadness. How had it come to this? Why did Alana have to go through this? Look how tiny she is. How is this gonna work? I looked on in shocked despair. Calming reassurance and clarity came in bucket loads from the medical staff, but no one would say it was going to be okay.

'She seems to be responding to the new ventilator,' said the doctor. 'Her saturation levels are up and they're stable again for now. That's positive. However, she is still critically ill.'

'Thank you,' I nodded, not able to draw my eyes away from Alana. I just wanted to scoop her up and love her, cuddle her in my big arms and smother her with love.

Please take care of her, please take care of her, please take care of her repeated in my head like a scratched record. Who I was begging to do this? It didn't register – nurses, doctors, God, anyone?

Keep it together, Gary, keep it together, I'd tell myself. *They said that it was helping her to breathe; that's good news. She's breathing better; that's great news. The ventilator's working; that's fabulous news.*

In my head, that meant that she was just as near to being ok as it was gonna get just now, but that was good enough for me. There was no way that I was gonna sit here and think anything else, be it for self-protection, naivety or whatever. She was breathing easier and that meant that maybe I could too.

A short time later, I was asked to leave again, but this time not to sit on the plastic chairs but to go home.

'Gary, you need to go home and get some rest,' a nurse told me. 'It's after 10pm. You've been on the go now for days. Alana will need you to have energy so go home, eat something and get some sleep. We'll ring you if we need you.'

It was so hard to go home. It just felt wrong and the longing in my heart was sore, but Paul said that he'd drop me home on his way home, too, so I agreed. We arranged for him to collect me the following morning and bring me back in, save me getting a taxi or having to park the car.

22

Home again to the same eerie quietness and the same emptiness. I put the TV on as a distraction; it was about the time of the Rugby World Cup of 2003, so the highlights were on. They were loud, and the noise of the crowd shouting and cheering filled the silence of the house. I drank some milk and the next thing I knew I woke with a colossal jolt, realising that I'd dropped off to sleep and feared that I'd missed a call from the hospital or from Michelle.

The screen was blank; no one had called. I had to take some deep breaths, my blood pressure shooting through the roof. I felt like I was living on a knife edge, my emotions and sense of exhaustion on overdrive. I wasn't sure how much more a body could take. I needed to get some rest, to regenerate a bit so I'd have enough energy to do the next day, and the one after that, and the ones that came after that.

I woke again at about 5am, feeling instantly sick with fear. There were still no missed calls, which I took as a positive, but I still didn't feel right. There was a feeling in my gut that was telling me this. I was so anxious to get back to Alana. I showered – my first since Thursday – to try and revive myself. The feeling remained. I decided that I needed to go in now, earlier that I'd planned with Paul, so I called a taxi and arrived back at the hospital for before 7am.

I could tell instantly that the atmosphere had changed. Nurse Michelle was back with Alana, but there was no banter and her bubbly personality was muted. She greeted me with the news that Alana was taking a turn for the worst, that although her oxygen levels had increased they were slipping again. I could feel the fear and the anger rising like lava, my head feeling like it would explode.

Why hadn't they told me? I'd have come in straight away. Why had I left in the first place? I was struggling to keep the anger down. I felt like the shittiest dad ever. I'd left her and now she wasn't doing well at all. It crucified me that I'd selfishly gone home for a sleep, a wash and some food. None of those was ere as important as being here with Alana, but I'd done it and now look what I'd come back to.

I wanted to blame the nurses and the doctors, to make it their fault that all of this was happening. The anger inside me was criticising them for letting this happen to Alana. I wanted Alana to get better again. That was all I was asking for. That was all I needed them to do and they weren't doing it. I couldn't see past the fact that they were trying everything in their medical power to help her. It wasn't working like any of us had hoped, but I still just wanted them to do more, try something else and make her better.

And then there was God again, that useless bastard! I blamed him, too. Not so powerful and almighty after all. He hadn't listened to my prayers either. When had he ever? He hadn't when I was a boy and he certainly wasn't listening now either. Bastard!

Paul arrived at about 8am. I was glad to have him around. He kept me going, kept me in drinks and a bit of banter every now and again, but we both knew that things weren't good. I'd spoke to Michelle on the way in, and late the night before, telling her how the ventilator was helping Alana. Dana was still doing okay, too, but now I knew that at some point I'd have to ring her again with entirely different news. Nurse Michelle said that the consultant would speak to me sometime that morning and I thought it'd be best to ring Michelle once he'd spoken to me.

What I heard or didn't hear when he arrived still baffles me today. It was too much, just all too much.

'Mr Anderson, we are very, very concerned about Alana this morning,' he said, sterned faced and sympathetic. 'There are many, many things that we are trying to support her with and...'

...and the list of things that were going wrong with her continued to reel out of his mouth, and seemed endless. It wasn't just her breathing; her heart obviously wasn't coping, the lack of oxygenated blood to her limbs and extremities meant that her circulation was poor and her leg was changing colour and was starting to die – the tips of her fingers, too. Potassium levels were mentioned and a whole crowd of other stuff. Oh Alana!

Fucking hell! Please stop! Please stop! I don't want to know anymore, I cried in my head, reeling from how devastating the words of the consultant were. How was she ever going to get better now? How could she recover from the list of stuff that I'd just been handed in words? I felt sick to the core of my core.

Were they telling me in no uncertain terms that she wasn't gonna make it? That there was no hope? Had all my praying and willing fallen on deaf ears yet again? She wasn't gonna make it. How could they be letting this happen? How could I be letting them think she wasn't gonna make it? There had to be more that they could do. I just couldn't comprehend what I was meant to be comprehending and didn't want to. It was just too much, too traumatising and too overwhelming. I couldn't think straight. I didn't know what to say. I didn't know what I was meant to do next, but I knew I wasn't gonna give up on her.

I knew I had to ring Michelle. Oh my God, how was I gonna tell her everything and her so far away? She shouldn't have had to hear about Alana over the phone.

The nurse said that I could use the telephone at the nurses' station. In fact, they made the phone call for me, because I was in a shock. By the time I spoke, the line was through to the ward that Michelle was on back in Shrewsbury. Nurse Michelle had written down on a piece of paper what was going on with Alana because I just didn't know what to say. The wait for Michelle to get to the phone was excruciating. The midwife on the other end had gone to fetch her, but it seemed to be taking ages.

I was finding it hard to keep my breathing under control. How was I going to find the strength and courage to read this list to Michelle? She was so, so far away from her little girl and things were look really grave. I knew that saying it out loud would make it more real. This was going to be the hardest telephone conversation I was ever going to make. Our baby girl was struggling in so many ways, was given little hope, and I didn't know what to do with it except what I'd always tried to do – keep hoping and believing that she was going to make it.

'Hiya, Gary, how's it going now? Is everything okay?' I could hear the nerves in Michelle's voice.

'The doctors have just spoken to me. Alana's not doing well, Bear.' The next set of words stuck in my throat. How was I gonna say them?

'The high-frequency ventilator is still doing the job, but her oxygen saturation levels keep dropping and they don't want to turn it up any higher. They said that her potassium levels are bad, too, but I'm not sure now. I couldn't take it all in. Her circulation is poor, too. Her little leg has turned blue, too, her right one.'

We were both crying now, the words making the situation even more real. Neither of us could speak for a bit because we were so choked with tears.

'There's not enough blood and oxygen circulating to stop it. They said they might have to amputate it.'

More tears, more silence while was were trying desperately to absorb the information. The list continued. It still felt endless. Every word still stuck in my throat on the way out.

'Oh Shelly, what are we gonna do?'

I could hear Michelle trying to control the sound of her sobbing on the other end of the phone and I couldn't hold back the sobs either. The moments of silent spoke volumes and neither of us wanted to say out loud that Alana might die soon if her condition didn't improve, and it seemed that it wasn't going to.

'I have to come, Gary. I have to come.' The sobbing continued. 'It's not looking good, is it? She's really poorly, isn't she?'

Both of us knew. Both of us acknowledged through our lack of words that we knew Alana was dying.

'I know, Tubby Bear, but they're trying everything they can.' I wanted to offer some sort of comfort to Michelle but doubted myself if the words were actually true. 'If they have to remove her leg then so be it. We can cope with that.' I felt so sick. I knew I was grabbing at straws, but didn't want to acknowledge anything else.

'Of course we can. I just need to come now. Mom and Dad are here, so I'll try and sort it with the nurses and get there as soon as I can.'

'What about Dana? How's she?' I knew that if things had also taken a turn for the worst with Dana, then Michelle would have found it incredibly difficult to leave her. How could she juggle two sick children?

'She's doing okay. Not much change really, still critical but stable. I still need to come. I need to see Alana.'

And at the word 'Alana', Michelle broke down further.

'Let me know what's happening then and I'll get in touch if I need to. Love you.'

'Love you, too.' And she was gone.

Fuck! Fuck! Fuck! I had no idea what Michelle was going to do or how she was going to do it, but I know she'd be doing all she could. I needed to get back in to Alana and let her know that her mummy was on her way. I worried for Michelle's journey – she was barely able to walk as it was – but I knew that no matter what, she'd come. She'd find a way and do what she needed to do.

23

The activity around Alana was now constant and there seemed to be people coming back and forth a lot, watching monitors and looking at charts. I stroked Alana's head gently with my finger, held her little hand and told her that her Mummy was on her way. I hoped that her knowing that her mummy was on the way would give her some encouragement to get better. Thinking like this kept the reality of what was happening at bay, but I couldn't hold it there for long. I knew I couldn't.

I looked on, feeling such hurt and pride. Alana had fought her whole life, from conception to now. She had such courage to keep going. She was doing her best to keep her little body alive and as long as she was fighting there was hope.

Come on, Michelle. Come on, Michelle.

I just wanted her to be here now. Alana was definitely deteriorating fast. I felt the fear and tension of being here without Michelle and the strong need to have her with me. She needed to be here. I wanted her to be here. Now. I also knew that her getting herself organised and here was no mean feat. Shrewsbury wasn't round the corner.

Time ticked by, but I had no conscious awareness of how many minutes or hours. I hoped Michelle wasn't going to be too long, as every minute now was so precious and I knew that not only was she missing minutes with Alana that I was getting, but also that future minutes might be short.

One of Michelle's family had organised a wheelchair for her for when she arrived, as we knew she would find it very difficult to walk from the front of the hospital to the ICU. After all, she'd just had an emergency twin Caesarean and her stress levels and blood pressure were really through the roof.

Her brother Paul and sister-in-law Caroline were at the main doors, waiting for Pat's car to stop in front and for her to get out. It must have been awful for them, too. It was breaking everybody's heart.

Dusk had arrived. I was standing leaning over Alana, talking to her, when I turned to see Michelle being wheeled into the ICU by her brother. When I looked up, the woman being wheeled towards me was already sobbing at the sight that met her, and as I walked towards her to hold her, and for her to hold me, deep, painful sobs came, sobs that knew what we were about to face.

My tears came thick and fast, too, no barrier strong enough to keep them in. We held each other for a long moment and let the sobs subside. We were back together again, here to support Alana with whatever was to come. For me, the hope that she'd live never left. I never let go of that thought. Together we stood over Alana's cot, just staring at her, and held her little hands as we did so. Bless her, her eyes were so vacant and yellow, her tiny chest was vibrating with the force of the ventilator and her limbs were lifeless. How was she going to come back from this? How was she going to make it?

Michelle removed Alana's blanket from her legs and exposed the extent of her blue leg, and the lack of circulation that was now smacking us in the face. Her poor leg was almost completely mottled-blue and clearly, there was going to be very little more that they could do with her leg except, inevitably, amputating it.

'The little tips of her fingers are going blue, too, Gary. Oh Alana! We love you so much.'

We were so helpless by her side. We could do nothing but stare and love her and pray for a miracle. The nurses were constantly there to make Alana as comfortable as possible and to monitor what the screens were telling them.

Soon after Michelle arrived, the consultants wanted to speak to use away from Alana, in a private room to discuss options and ways forward. The room was directly adjacent to the family room and as I wheeled Michelle in I saw that her family were there, all ready to support and be there for her and for Alana. They were there for me, too, but I didn't realise that. I didn't know. It didn't really enter my consciousness. I was the new guy on the block. They'd only known me for four years and getting to know me was no easy feat, even on a good day.

My own family hadn't cared for me, so I had no expectation that Michelle's family would have picked up where my own had left off. I wouldn't have thought about their care for me, I just wanted them to care for Michelle and really thought that that was why they were there. Of course, nothing could have been further from the truth.

They were going through this pain with us, as a couple, alongside us, willing Alana to live like we were.

The consultant spoke a lot of words that fogged together. I just wanted to hear that she was going to live, that she was going to get over this blip and start to get well again, but I wasn't hearing those words. I wasn't hearing *any* words, but I got the tone and it wasn't good. I could feel the frustration and desperation beginning to mount within me with every moment that passed.

'But she can make it, can't she?' I blurted out, wanting to pull the words that I wanted to hear out of the doctor's mouth – positive, reassuring words of certain hope.

'She is critical. There may become a point that we won't be able to help her any further.'

There was a pause, a heavy gap that said so many words.

'However, we do have one drug that may support her a little more and ease the strain on her heart. The side effects of the drug, though, would mean that the toxins in her leg would practically be flushed around her body. This in itself has many dangers. The toxins would flow into her blood stream and this could result in us losing her, too.'

'Well, if there's something that you can try, we have to try it!' I blurted out again.

I was never going to give up on my little girl and I was certainly not going to let them either. The pain of desperation filled my chest and I just wanted to yell at the top of my lungs: 'Save her! For fuck's sake, just fucking save her!'

More words came from the consultant about getting the drug from pharmacy and the time that might take, but I wasn't interested in the logistics. The drug would come and Alana would improve. My thoughts were panicked and terrifying, real thoughts lost in a fog of words and emotion.

'If you think she's about to die, will you make sure that we are there with her, please?' said Michelle, such sorrowful words from a mum about her dying child. 'Don't let her die on her own without us, please!'

'Of course. We'll make sure that we keep you as updated as possible. We'll order the drug now and let you know when it arrives. Do you have any further questions at this point?'

91

Questions? Questions? I had millions of fucking questions, but they were all jumbled up inside my jumbled head. Most couldn't have been answered in this room anyway. My little girl was dying. I wanted someone to tell me why her, why me, why us. We'd been through enough and here we were, listening to what felt like the end of the road for Alana.

Please, God, let them be wrong. Please! Please! Let them be wrong, I screamed, silently. *She's only tiny, give her a chance. She hasn't lived a life yet!*

All sorts of thoughts shot in and out of my head, none making any sense, whizzing and whirling, and some cut short by the intrusion of others pushing passed. What the hell was I supposed to do now? Just sit and wait? Was I waiting for Alana to get better? Get worse? Was I to sit with her and just love her to death – literally? There was so much telling me that she was extremely ill and there was going to be no coming back from it, but the heartache of even considering that she might die was just unthinkable. I was definitely not going to give up believing that things would be ok. I was only just beginning to get to know Alana. I wasn't willing to let her go.

On our way back to being with Alana, Michelle asked to be wheeled in to see her own family in the relatives' room, directly next to where we'd just left, so that she could let them know what was happening and where we were at.

Her parents, her siblings, their partners, all there to support us and Alana at such a crucial time, had put their own family lives on hold. Between them all there were nine other nieces and nephews at home or somewhere else being looked after by someone else, because their parents were looking after their Aunty Michelle, Uncle Gary and cousin Alana.

Her family were all very tearful, knowing that the situation was so grave and just having Michelle wheeled in made the tears flow in abundance. How she was able to speak and relay what the doctors had just said is beyond me, but she did. She was so distraught, the intensity of the reality coming out of her mouth so real.

'Please pray for her,' she continued through her sobbing. 'Please pray to family in heaven to look after her if she dies. Pray to Nanny and ask Katherine to look after her for me 'til I get there.'

Everyone nodded and cried and as quick as she'd entered, she left and we were heading back along the ICU corridor to Alana.

The 'last chance' drug had still not arrived. There were loads of medical staff around Alana at different points and she was looking even more poorly and hollow-eyed. I cannot express how much love I had for her, how much my heart was breaking and my world was falling apart. Myself and Michelle stood with her, looking at her and loving her, constantly. There were so many beeps and noises coming from the machines that surrounded her, echoing like sirens in my head, and doctors looking back and forth between the screens and Alana as they did their best to keep her alive.

'She's bradycardic!' I heard one of the doctor's shout. Alana's heart rate had plummeted to almost nothing.

Oh my God, she's really going to die on me, right here in front of my eyes.

We held each other as we looked on in shock and disbelief but within seconds, her heart rate rose and she was back with us again, a reprieve in such panic.

Come on, Alana, you can do this! I cried inside.

But within minutes, the doctor who was listening to Alana's chest looked up at both of us and said,

'I'm so sorry. She's got blood in her lungs.'

I could hear the wail escape from Michelle's mouth and the sharp intake of sorrowful breath.

'Please stop now! Please don't do anymore! Don't put her through anymore. Please let her just be with her Mommy and Daddy,' Michelle cried and there were no words needed in response.

Oh my God, Alana Bear was actually going to die, right here, right now. I clung to Michelle and she to me. We grabbed each other in utter despair, trying to make eye contact but knowing that it was too painful to do so, looking instead at the doctors who were disconnecting Alana from beeps and wires.

'Can she die with us?'

'Of course.'

I could barely breathe; my lungs were in survival mode. The pains across my chest were stabbing, crushing and spreading. Oh God, she's gonna die! She's gonna die! Surely, they can do more? Surely this isn't the end? Already? She'd only just been given life and already it was ending.

This wasn't the way it was meant to be. This wasn't right. Excruciating sorrow enveloped me. I wanted to scream out loud the thoughts in my head: *Please don't give up on her! Come on, do something else! Keep trying!* I didn't want to believe that this was the end of her short life.

Still ventilating Alana manually, they handed her tiny, tired body to Michelle. The three of us sat together in a huddle, Michelle cradling her dying child and me cradling them both. In another life, we would have resembled the nativity scene, but this was now and we were holding our beautiful baby girl while she passed away.

'You can rest now, Alana, you don't have to fight anymore,' Michelle repeated over and over again while kissing Alana's tiny face.

We cried and huddled and were unable to do anything else besides simply try and value the last moments that we were going to have with her, her last breaths. These moments were so, so precious to us, ones filled with indescribable pain and despair.

The only words that came from my mouth repeatedly were, 'I love you so much, Alana. I love you.'

The doctor told us that he was going to stop the manual ventilation and we were given time to hold Alana as she took her last breaths. We sat with her, holding her and loving her for a further twenty minutes or so, while the doctor periodically listened to Alana's chest to see if she was still breathing. Every time, there was still a faint heartbeat, small and fragile, but still there. She was still with us and still fighting, bless her. Maybe our love was keeping her alive for an extra few minutes. We cuddled her and spoke to her constantly for a short while longer and then the words came that nobody should ever hear about their own child.

'I can't hear her heartbeat anymore.' the doctor nodded, 'She's gone.'

My Little Bear Alana died at 6.30pm on Sunday October 19th 2003. She was three days old.

24

I have never been so broken-hearted.

There are no words in our language that can express the loss.

'I wanted to have so much fun with you!' I cried to her as I held her little limp body close to mine, feeling the intense loss of the future that I'd planned and hoped for with her.

I wanted to be her dad – to play with her, play jokes on her, watch her grow, tell her off when her bedroom looked like a bomb site, vet her boyfriends and walk her down the aisle. All that was gone now. All my hopes and dreams with her had been shattered there and then, taken when Alana's life was taken. What were we going to do now?

The pain and helplessness was all-consuming, heavy and drenching. I cuddled her and cuddled her, hugging her through the blankets that swaddled her, wanting to keep her warm but knowing that the life inside her was already gone and my warmth was fruitless. That didn't matter; she was my little girl and I was going to hold her, love her, care for her and talk to her for as long as someone would let me. All the bleeping stopped and the wires were removed. She looked just like a sleeping, angelic baby, but there was no life left. She wasn't asleep.

We sat with Alana for a long time, just being with her. I couldn't take my eyes off her – I didn't want to anyway, ever. I looked on as Michelle cradled her in her arms. Michelle had been born eleven weeks premature herself and fought through many things in her life, but here she was now, holding her own premature daughter who hadn't been able to pull through like she had. Alana had fought on 'til her mummy had arrived. I truly believed that.

Her mummy had got here in time to hug her precious baby girl while she was still alive, but it was heart-breaking that her first hug with her daughter was when the doctor handed Alana to her to die. It was all so cruel. If there was a heaven – and I wasn't sure what I believed – Alana would be there now, knowing how much her mummy and daddy loved her and had held her while she died, and knowing that so many other people loved her, too.

Michelle's brother Paul had been with us the whole time. How he kept it together in our sight I don't know. Michelle's family came in to say their goodbyes to Alana, to see her at peace. Everyone was devastated. They'd lost a member of their family, too.

It overwhelmed my already saturated mind that they felt it okay to come in. These moments for me were private. I was at the lowest point in my life and felt the excruciating pain of grief and vulnerability. I didn't want to be looked at by others. I wanted Alana to myself, to allow this time to pass just with her, just for me and Michelle, not for visitors. Of course, I knew that they weren't visiting and that they just wanted to give her a kiss and say their goodbyes to her, but it felt intrusive. I wasn't used to having my own family around in good times, let alone bad, so it all felt too much for me to accept. It felt wrong. I wanted to scream out loud to them, irrationally, irritated, 'Leave us alone!'

Somewhere inside me I knew that we were only going to be allowed to keep Alana with us for a short amount of time and I selfishly wanted to keep all of those precious seconds and minutes for myself, but their granddaughter had just died, too, their niece. All of them were ultra-respectful and only came to give Alana a kiss and us a kiss and to say goodbye before they left to go home to their own families. It was barely a few minutes really, but it did feel intrusive on my time with my daughter.

I wasn't angry at them, though. I was angry at my own lack of family. No matter how much support Michelle's family gave me, the lack of presence from my own family only cemented how lonely in life I felt. I just couldn't accept the love and sorrow that another family were feeling. Would I even ring to tell my mum or dad to tell them what had been going on? Here was I, cradling my dead daughter, bursting with love for her and realising that this was how you were meant to feel when you had a child – love that was all consuming, unconditional, endless, everything.

My parents had been shit at all of those things! How dare they! They'd been given the opportunity to love and nurture me when I was born, but had failed dramatically. I'd followed in their footsteps until treatment told me otherwise. I was angry inside, really angry. I knew how much I loved Alana and would have given my every breath to bring her back and my parents had taken the gift of me, their child, for granted. The bastards! Why hadn't they loved me like I loved Alana? What had been so wrong with me as a child?

25

It takes a special kind of person to be a children's nurse and Nurse Michelle was amazing, with Alana and with me and Michelle. As serious as everything was and as devastated as we were, there was also a sense of calm, thanks to having Nurse Michelle around us.

'I'll take a few photographs of you as a family as a keepsake for you,' she said to us. 'Something for yourselves, and something for Dana to have when she grows up.'

Photos? Now? As much as I was desperate for her to take the photographs, it just felt so wrong. I mean, who takes photographs of dead children? It seemed so wrong, but then I'd lost track of what was right and what wasn't. It's hard not to automatically pose or look at a camera when it's pointing at you, but that was the last thing that I wanted to be doing.

I'm sure 'Joe Public' might have comments to say about taking photos of a dead child with their parents. Nowadays, the righteous judge and jury of social media might have a field day, but I didn't care what anyone thought, 'Joe Public' or otherwise. I wanted the photos; I wanted whatever anyone could offer me that would keep Alana close to me.

We were making memories now, excruciating, difficult, surreal memories, but precious nevertheless. These wouldn't be photos to be placed on the mantelpiece or blown up large on a canvas and hung proudly on a wall in our hallway. Not even placed in a photo album along with the holiday snaps. No, these would be private photos for me, Michelle and maybe Dana when she was older, photographs that I would treasure and know that when I looked at them I'd see myself holding Alana again, just one more time. My little Alana, my Little Bear.

'If you'd like to, you can wash Alana and dress her in fresh clothes,' said Nurse Michelle.

'Yes, we'd like that,' we replied together. This was another surreal question, with an equally surreal answer. We were going to give our daughter her first wash, the only one we'd ever give her. Again, it must sound completely weird to someone who has never been in that situation, but this was all we had, a small task that we could do with Alana as her mummy and daddy. We'd never get the chance again.

'We can also take her hand and footprints, too,' said Nurse Michelle. 'You can have them to keep.'

'That'd be lovely, thank you. How do you do them?' we asked.

'We have special paint that we roll on to her hands and feet and then we print them on to paper,' she explained. 'We'll put them in a little booklet for you with her other things.'

Handprints and footprints. Hands that I'd never hold, feet that I'd never tickle.

I was so delicate with her when the time came to wash Alana, wanting to do an honourable job. This was such a simple job in everyday life to the rest of the world, but such a responsibility in my here and now. We used little cotton buds and cotton wool dipped in warm water, in smooth, gentle strokes that barely touched her delicate skin. Tears were rolling down our cheeks as we did so. In every moment, we couldn't believe that this was real and that we were the family living this nightmare.

Patrick and Caroline had bought beautiful outfits as gifts for Alana and Dana, and we were happy to use one of them to dress Alana in. It was a yellow sleepsuit with the slogan, 'Good things come in small packages' written across the chest, with a tiny, yellow hat to match. Never a truer word said.

We dressed her careful with the support of Nurse Michelle, and cuddled her in a blanket that was also a gift. She looked so cosy and warm, snug in her new clothes and blanket like she was just sleeping. It was so hard to believe that she was dead; she didn't look it or feel it. Michelle's family also sent in a holy medal to put with her. I didn't mind. It didn't mean anything to me, but Michelle was happy that Alana had it.

More photos were taken, not many but enough that we had our memories. Again, it was just so surreal. Nurse Michelle gave us two envelopes, each containing booklets of Alana's tiny things – one for us, one for Dana. Each booklet had Alana's name and birthday on the front and inside were the photos that had been taken earlier, her hand and footprints, her hospital name tags from her incubator, and her tiny, woollen hat, such precious objects for such a precious little girl.

I left Michelle and Alana for a few minutes to phone Michael, I remember the clock on the wall telling me that it was almost 7pm. As I've said, Michael is family to me, and I just wanted to ring him, but the silence on the other end of the phone told it all. The truth was we were both too lost for words to say anything. Intense loneliness engulfed me. I was lonely for the family that had no clue of the tragedy I was dealing with, and lonely because I was surrounded by another family whose obvious interest was primarily Michelle, but who I couldn't let in even if I tried. I just needed someone here that belonged to me, who would be here for me, who knew me for what I was and how totally devastated I was right in this moment. I wanted Michael to be here in Birmingham, but knew that he was half a dozen hours away back in my home town. I knew he wanted to be here with me, too. I said I'd phone him when we were heading back to Shrewsbury. I didn't know when that'd be. I didn't want to leave Alana, not ever.

Michelle was cradling Alana when I got back. In such tragedy, it's hard to believe that there are moments when you smile and laugh, but there are. It's just being human, I guess. I remember laughing through tears when Nurse Michelle produced the scary doll I'd bought for Alana the day before. It was underneath her incubator now. Michelle hadn't seen it yet, of course.

'Are you ready for this?' Nurse Michelle said.

We all burst out laughing when she pulled it out to show my Michelle.

'Oh my God, where on earth did you get that from?' Michelle laughed, spontaneously. She looked at me straight in the face trying to get some sort of sense from it.

'Let me explain,' I laughed, knowing that my explanation would make her laugh even more. I couldn't defend myself, it really was a shocking doll. 'I bought it without realising what it looked like. I just saw the pink face and thought it was okay. You can tell what sort of a hurry I was in and where my head was at!'

'It looks scary! I'm glad Alana didn't see it. It would've made her jump out of her skin!'

'I know. I didn't want to say anything to him when he brought it in!' Even the nurse was laughing loudly with us. 'That's why I left it under the incubator today!'

With that, the Highland log-thrower became known as Scary Doll for all time. She had brought us a rare moment of humour during the desperate time that we were living in.

26

I knew the time would come for us to have to leave Alana, but I didn't want to acknowledge it. I didn't want to let her go. The doctors who had certified her death came to speak to us once more. Thinking back, we take it for granted that medical staff look after the needs of the patient, but it goes way, way beyond that. I wasn't the patient, I was further down the ripple effect; but we were cared for with such respect and dignity.

We were asked whether we would like to organise our own funeral or whether we needed the hospital to organise the funeral internally. Apparently that was possible.

'Thank you, but we'd want to organise that ourselves,' I said.

A funeral hadn't even crossed my mind, but I instantly knew that it was something I wanted to organise myself. It was too important to me to hand it over to someone else. It was Nurse Michelle that told us what would happen next.

'We have Rainbow Rooms here at the hospital. They're rooms where you can bring Alana and spend time with her for as long as you need to.'

It sounded like the right thing, but, again, I'd never contemplated that hospitals needed such a place – but of course they do. I was completely absorbed in my own grief and uncertainty and I bet there were many, many more sets of parents around the hospital going through exactly the same thing at the death of their child. Birmingham Children's Hospital deals with death on a daily if not hourly basis. This wasn't exclusive to me, though it felt like it at the time.

'We can wrap her in her lovely blanket and you can carry her to the Rainbow Rooms, if that is what you'd like to do.'

'I'd like that,' I said, choked up again.

Another surreal moment: being asked to carry your dead child through hospital corridors. I felt honoured and privileged to be carrying my little girl, however. Michelle wrapped her tiny body in her beautiful blanket and I took Alana from her. Michelle had to sit back in the wheelchair that they'd provided earlier, but I held Alana close to my chest, the weight of the blanket heavier that the weight of her body.

It was getting later in the evening now, but, as hospitals never sleep, there were still plenty of people mulling around in the corridors, coming, going and working. Feeling honoured was soon overtaken with the fear and knowledge that I was holding my dead daughter. Would it show in my face? Would people instantly know that that's what I was doing?

Michelle's parents were waiting at the end of the ICU corridor. Michelle had wanted them to go home, but they had waited; after all, Michelle was still their 'baby' and Alana their granddaughter. We left the ICU and continued to walk. No one stopped us, no one asked questions and no one stared. I was just a dad holding his baby and, to the outside world, that is exactly what it looked like: a cute, tiny baby, wrapped in a blanket, held by her doting dad.

As we walked, the corridors became less busy, with the hum of human life fading away. The final corridor felt instantly cold as I walked along it, I could tell that we were no longer in the hub of the building, but near the outskirts. I could feel my heart beating out of my chest in anticipation of the time ahead. Nurse Michelle was with us and showed us into one of the Rainbow Rooms. It had been laid out ready for us.

There was a single bed in there, and in front of a two-seater settee was a beautiful baby's crib – a wicker one – with delicate broderie anglaise covers. I'd seen plenty of this type of crib before in people's houses and never given them a second thought, but here, now, the crib was full of significance and it drew me in. I knew that this was the place I'd have to leave Alana, my special girl, my Little Bear, my angel in heaven. I carried Alana in and the three of us sat together on the settee.

'You can stay as long as you need to,' Nurse Michelle said, gently.

'Is this where we leave Alana?' I said. 'Just here?' I indicated the crib.

'Yes, when you're ready.'

'What happens then? Where will she go?' I felt panicked.

'I'll stay with her and take her to the mortuary for you,' came the nurse's reply. Bless her, I'm sure this wasn't the easiest part of her job description.

So here we were, sitting with Alana, knowing that we were going to have to let her go. I didn't know how I was going to do it. In fact, I had to fight the enormous feeling to rebel and not let her go at all.

'I just want to take her home,' I said. 'I don't want to leave her here. I don't want to leave her on her own.'

'I know, Gary, but that's the way it has to be.' Michelle said, feeling the same as me but keeping reality in check. Where she got her strength from, I have no idea.

We sat on the settee and cried and loved Alana as much as we could, trying to fill her lost soul with the years and years of love that we had stored inside of us, just for her. How could we manage that or even contemplate it?

People always say that there's an instant love like no other when your children are born, and they're right. The love I felt for the twins, and right now for Alana especially, was all consuming and intense. I'd never experienced anything like it. Had this been five, 10, 15 or even 20 years earlier, my failing mental health wouldn't have allowed me to feel such a thing as this love. I loved Michelle so much, but even that love wasn't a patch on the love that I felt now – and worse still, it was a heartbroken love that only made the hurt worse.

After what must have been about another half-hour or so, I knew that it was coming close to the inevitable. 'We need to go soon, Gary. We've still got to get back to Shrewsbury,' Michelle reasoned.

Little Dana Bear was there surviving all alone now, no parents and no sister. I knew we needed to get back to her too. We had our last cuddles together and told Alana how much we loved her.

'Sleep now, Little Bear. See you in heaven,' Michelle's voice no more than a whisper.

Michelle carefully lowered Alana into the beautiful crib and covered her further with the pretty, white, quilted blanket that was there. The need to keep her warm, protected, safe, was overwhelming. It was silly really – or not. Even her being away from our bodies and looking down on her in the crib, she was too far away from me. She may as well have been a mile away, let alone just a few feet. How was I going to leave her? I couldn't, just couldn't.

'They'll look after her, Gary. We'll be able to see her again. We can visit her again.'

104

We stood and kissed our Little Bear and somehow my feet walked me out of that room. I felt cold as the door was shut behind her and us, and the reality hit me that she was gone, really gone. The temptation to turn back, grab her and take her with me was so powerful.

It's those around you who give the instructions to walk in the opposite direction to where your heart wants to go and keep going. We were leaving the hospital, the place where Alana was alone without her parents. How was I gonna do it? I remember the cold air hitting my skin as we walked out of the main entrance of the hospital. It was busy – the A&E is right next to where we were, Steel House Lane police station is directly across the road, and the ambulance station is next to the walkway.

I saw life around me was going on – people going on nights out, others coming to visit sick children in the hospital, criminals being charged, roads full of headlights and horns. Had any of them just held their child while she died? Was it just me? Could they tell from my face that I was a heartbroken dad who'd just left his dead daughter in the mortuary?

My thoughts were crisscrossing between heartbreak, fear and numbness as I climbed into Michelle's brother's car. He was taking us on the long ride back to Shrewsbury, back to Dana. Poor little Dana Bear. She'd spent her whole life next to her little sister Alana, and now she'd never get to know her or remember being with her. Bless her, I'd make sure I'd tell her everything I knew, every minute that I remembered spending with Alana.

Then another jolt of panic hit me: what if Dana dies too? What if she didn't make it? What if I had to do all this again? Once more, I was dealing with the thought that karma had eventually caught up with me, and this was my punishment for all the bad things I'd done when I was younger, that it was punishment for all the people I'd hurt along the way, ones I'd let down, been nasty to, held grudges against and been violent to. Was this all my fault? Was one of my daughter's dead and the other still in a critical state because of me? How could it not be? Michelle had lived a good life. She hadn't done anything bad to anyone, so it had to be me, it had to be my fault. No one else could be to blame.

Tears of shame, anger and guilt came, hard and hot, but I knew that this wasn't gonna be the time or the place to do this, if I'd ever really let myself do it. I sunk the emotion back inside, cross at myself for my selfish thoughts and feelings when I should have just been thinking about Alana, Dana and Michelle.

27

We knew the journey back to Shrewsbury would be about an hour or so, and Paul was very good at making sure we were okay – whatever being 'okay' now meant.

'When was the last time you ate, you two?' he said as he pulled away.

'God knows,' I said. I hadn't a clue. Had I eaten breakfast? I couldn't recall; I couldn't remember anything.

Not only was it getting late to find somewhere to get food, but it was also a late Sunday night, so the options were really limited. I wasn't bothered. Food wasn't something that'd crossed my mind.

'You both need to eat something. There won't be anything open at the hospital. I'll find somewhere to stop and get chips or something.' I'm guessing Paul hadn't eaten all day either and must have been starving.

He drove to our familiar chip shop on the way to the motorway junction, but it was shut so he diverted off the path and found another within a mile. We caught the chippy as it was shutting. The three of us sat picking at chips in the warmth of the car.

What was I doing? My daughter had just died and here I was, picking at chips! What the fuck! Logically, I was listening to Paul who was telling me that I needed to eat something and nodding because I knew it was an autopilot, sensible response, but there was the other side of me that was feeling so fucking disrespectful for sitting eating bloody chips with my dead daughter lying in the mortuary only a few miles down the road. What was I doing?

There were so many conflicting emotions, all piling in, hankering for space, that I didn't know one end of me from the other. Incidentally, the chips went cold and were thrown out to the bins, papers still full, before we continued our journey onwards.

We didn't talk much. What was there to say? I wasn't even sure if I thought much either, other than the fact that I'd left Alana all alone and the guilt and sadness that sat with me.

Michelle was very anxious about what had just happened and anxious, too, about what we'd find when we got back to Shrewsbury. What if Dana had taken a turn for the worst while we'd been away? We'd spoken to the ward to check on how she was, but that was hours ago. So much could happen in a few hours; so much already had. What if she was dying, too? What if we got there and they told us that she'd taken a turn for the worse and that she was going to die? What if she was already dead?

So many thoughts came from so many angles that it was impossible to shift them aside, and no manner of reassurance from anyone would have made any difference. If one daughter was dead, then why was it not possible that the other could be dead, too? The thoughts were crippling.

As much as we were desperate to get back to Dana, there was something within me that actually didn't want to get back, in case the reality of her criticalness was too much to bear. I mean, how much more could I take? If we walked into the Neonatal Unit and they told us that Dana's condition had worsened and was in danger of dying, how would I be able to take that? Only hours before, I'd already lived the same nightmare. There was no more mental space in my head to take anymore. There was another thought: poor little Dana, lying there all alone without anyone who truly loved her. Please God she hasn't had to deal with anything new while we'd been away. Please just let her be the same or better.

It was after 10pm when Paul dropped us at the doors of the maternity unit and headed home. He had to work the next day and still had the drive all the way back to Birmingham. I'm not sure how he kept going either.

We went straight through into the Neonatal Unit. I was dreading it. I also knew that the staff inside would have heard about Alana's death and I didn't want them to give me any hollow sympathy. That would make me angry, but to attach my anger to them would be wrong. I was angry with life, angry that my daughter had been taken away from me before she'd had a chance to live. It wasn't their fault, but didn't care that they'd be my excuse to act that way.

As it happened, they were the total opposite. They gently took Michelle in, sympathised briefly and brought us to Dana's incubator. I followed, glad that the attention was on Michelle and not me. I couldn't have handled it, even if I had wanted it. Michelle was my and their priority and that suited me just fine for now.

The outpouring of grief as Michelle stood at Dana's incubator was heart-breaking and painful. No one spoke, and in the quietness of the ward late at night, the cries echoed louder. She was practically hugging Dana's incubator, desperately wanting to get Dana out, desperate to hold her and for any degree of comfort. No one stopped her or tried to make her sit down. I stood with her and we all just stared, and let it happen. Here I was, back in another hospital, staring at a baby identical to the one that I'd left, dead, in another hospital. Their identicalness still startled me every time I thought about them. Now I had a different picture in my head of them: one alive, one dead, but still identical.

We were relieved to hear that Dana was still doing okay. She was critical but stable. She had her little CPAP oxygen mask on and wires galore, but she was okay for now. Such relief.

We sat with Dana and were handed cups of tea, but I have no idea what was said or who was there. Dana was here but Alana wasn't. Nothing else went round in my head. The last time I'd been sitting here, Alana's incubator had been right next to Dana's. Now there was an empty incubator, dull and clinical, waiting for its next occupant. Alana should have been there. It was her space. Dana's incubator looked lonely without her.

There were no other babies in the ICU part of the unit to keep her company. She was alone here now, alone without other babies around her and alone forever without her twin sister.

28

Meanwhile, Michelle still needed to be looked after because of her caesarean, so we went back to her ward and to the room she'd packed up and left earlier. It was all so surreal. Just a few days ago, I'd sat on the same settee and spoken about popping back and forth to see Alana and Dana in the neonatal ward, but Alana was gone now, forever.

Michelle's blood pressure was sky high when it was checked. Every 15 minutes the nurse would arrive again to retake it. They were worried. 'Try and rest, Michelle. Try and keep yourself as calm as you can. I know that's very difficult in the circumstances, but please try.'

Were they having a laugh? She'd not long held her baby daughter in her arms as she died and they wanted her to be calm and rest? Potentially, if her blood pressure didn't start to shift down soon, it was a heart attack or a stroke waiting to happen. I know drugs were mentioned, but they were reluctant to give any as they also wanted breast milk from Michelle to feed Dana; but the option of not having to give her some were getting slimmer.

'I'm gonna try, I'm gonna try,' was all Michelle could offer.

By now it was probably well into the middle of the night. I was suddenly jolted by the ringtone of my mobile phone: it was Michael. I could tell that he was in his car, but what I didn't know was that he'd jumped in the car when he'd heard the news about Alana and was in Shrewsbury, trying to find his way to the hospital. I couldn't believe it.

It overwhelmed me and left me speechless to think that he'd come all this way, hours of driving, to be with me and Michelle. I hadn't expected it or ever thought it. This was beyond kindness in my world. He wasn't my biological family, but he was as near as it could be in my eyes.

In the sadness, we joked about him not being able to find the hospital. He was asking me how to get here – me, a non-local who had turned up in Shrewsbury, unexpectedly, a few days before, and had not been anywhere other than the hospital; don't forget, these were the days before the convenience of satnav on your iPhone. I think I actually asked one of the nurses on the ward to help him because I was as lost as he was.

I went out to the entrance to wait for him coming. I didn't know how I was gonna handle it when he arrived. We were both tough, northern blokes who weren't renowned for showing how we felt or for knowing the right words to say.

When he arrived, parked up, and then spotted me waiting for him, his words were simple, and to the point: 'I'm so sorry, mate.'

Those words were enough. Michael shook my hand and we stood in the entrance, full of emotion, not knowing what else to say. Emotion was willing itself out of both of us, but couldn't escape. That was just not how things were done between us, but an expectation carried through from growing up.

We both knew the immense tragedy of the situation, and the feelings and emotions that we both had, but the words were scarce. I even think that it would have been easier for us both to have had such an emotion-filled conversation with a complete stranger than it was having one together. Talking to a stranger would mean nothing; it would keep the emotion calmer.

Whatever we could or couldn't say to each other, having Michael here now meant everything. Someone was here who knew me more than anyone else in the world, probably more than Michelle did. He was someone I could depend on, someone who wouldn't judge me, someone who had no expectations of me and accepted me for me.

His being here didn't need words or gestures, it was just everything I needed. Having said all that, it is reflecting that gives you the insight and words to express what moments in time felt like, but at the time, standing in the entrance to the maternity unit, there was a certain sense of awkwardness between us.

He was my best mate, my family, but in such a time of immense grief neither of us knew what to do. So we did what many men would have done and diverted away from the extremity of the situation and made small talk.

'So, did you stop and ask for directions in the end to get here, then?'

'Nah, I made it here myself.'

We both laughed a bit to ease the tension a little. I knew the answer to the question before I'd even asked him. There was no way that Michael would have asked for directions and there was no way that I would have done either. We were so similar. We'd rather roam around for hours looking ourselves than to admit that we needed help from someone else. Like me, he'd eventually get to where he was going, but the detour and the stubbornness could easily add an hour or so on to your journey. Silence soon came crawling back though.

'I don't know what to say, mate. I don't know what to say. What can I say?'

'I know, Mick.'

More silence.

'Come in. Michelle's got a room on the ward.'

We started to walk.

'I've told them that you're my brother, otherwise they won't let you in.' Anyway, he was a brother to me.

When we got to the room, all three of us still didn't know what to say to each other. There was just a background noise of tears and snivels. Michelle left with the midwife to go to the room next door to see if she could express milk. I felt so sorry for her, she could barely walk, was in pain, her blood pressure was through the roof and now she had to express milk while sitting sobbing about her dead child and another who was unwell. Fucking unreal.

Me and Mick sat there and began to talk about random stuff with very little content. It was meaningless, intermittent chatter, but it was what I needed. Michael has a great way of making you laugh and is happy to be the butt of his own jokes. It helped to hear him doing that here, now, but in the silence that followed, my thoughts were straight back to where I was and why I was here. I couldn't stop thinking about little Alana and what had happened to her poor, wee body. Could we have done more? Could they have done more? Did they get it wrong? It was pure torture.

'I'm gonna have to do that registration thing about her dying, Mick. I'm gonna have to register her death.'

'I'll come with you. I can stay as long as you want.'

Amazing friend.

'We haven't even registered her birth yet, man. Fuck's sake!'

It was too much to take in. Registering children's births was meant to be a joyous occasion. Registering a death wasn't. Neither would be joyous in my case. It was all so fucked up and wrong.

Mick made coffee. We drank it quickly and then had another one straight afterwards. It was something to do. There was a vending machine in the reception area so we took a walk there while we waited for Michelle to come back. It was hard to just sit there in our thoughts.

She seemed to have been gone for ages, and it was a relief when she returned.

'How did it go?' I asked, relieved that she was back and the pressure was off me in some way.

'Nothing came out.'

'Nothing at all?'

'No nothing at all.'

This added to her upset. Her breasts were so engorged, but the milk just wouldn't flow.

'It's just the stress of everything,' the midwife reassured us. 'It will start to flow eventually, but for now, because it won't, but needs to; you will have to syphon the milk off. We'll get you to lie in the bath every few hours to do that.'

I was at such loss at what to do. Everything that I was experiencing was completely out of my remit. It was like being thrown in front of a new bus every few hours, at the same time Michelle's medical needs strangely meant that we were almost 'occupied' for a while, be it on autopilot. I know that I spent much of my time staring into space.

'Can Michael stay with us tonight? He's travelled through the night to get here,' I pleaded with the nurse.

'Sure, he can stay tonight.'

I didn't correct the nurse when she talked about him as my brother. They gave him a bit of bedding to keep him warm and he slept on the floor of Michelle's room. I lay on the settee. Sleep came on and off out of pure exhaustion, but I know it didn't come for Michelle. Besides, she was still being checked all of the time and

every few hours she was having yet another bath to syphon off milk
that she desperately wanted to save for Dana, but couldn't.

29

I must have dropped off to sleep, because before I knew it, it was a new morning. Day one without Alana. The only words that come to mind to describe how I felt are 'despairing functionality'. I brushed my teeth, ate a piece of toast, drank a cup of tea, cried.

Nothing else happened, as my thoughts were so absorbed with Alana's death. I had such a feeling of injustice along with every other feeling. This shouldn't have happened. Babies weren't born to die. The amount of 'what if' conversations I had in my head was excessive. What if the ambulance had driven faster or been a bit earlier? What if there'd been cots in Birmingham instead of having to come to Shrewsbury? I wanted there to be a reason for such tragedy, so I had a way of blaming something or someone other than myself.

If I'd been an upstanding citizen all my life, I bet this wouldn't have happened, I taunted myself.

Guilt, such guilt.

I even felt guilty about the fact that I'd had the cheek to think about having any type of dreams or expectations about my future with Alana. Who did I think I was? Who was I to think that I deserved goodness – not just any goodness, the all-consuming goodness of a beautiful baby girl, a daughter – when I'd treated others so poorly in the past? Who was I kidding? If I'd had a choice, there and then, I'd have gone with Alana. I didn't want to be here. Surely death was better than what I was feeling? At least death would be a release for me, a way out of the pain.

Stop being such a selfish bastard! I'd then think to myself with distaste, instantly contradicting myself. *Alana would have given anything to be breathing like you, and now you're thinking about throwing your life away. You selfish fucker!*

I knew I wasn't going to do it, I wasn't going to take my own life, but that didn't stop the want to do it. It was only the stark reality of Dana and Michelle that held my dishevelled mind and soul together.

I needed to get out for some fresh air and get away from myself, my grief, my worry, my guilt, my everything.

I decided to ring my mum and dad. To this day I still do not fully understand what possessed me to do it or why I felt it was something that I wanted to do. In my average day, they'd be the last people I'd want to speak to. So why now? A little boy yearning for his parents? A cry for help? A cry for acceptance? A realisation that children were such a beautiful blessing and I'd never felt that from them, but still hoped I'd get?

Surely in this most tragic time, they'd respond to me with the love that I needed? I saw Michelle's family rallying round and doing whatever they could to help and support us.

My parents didn't know that the Bears had even been born, let alone that Alana had died yesterday. They'd separated when I was young and both remarried, and since then I'd gone through lots of different stints of being in contact with them and then not speaking to them for years. They'd met Michelle – we'd stayed with both of them a few years passed – but everything about my relationship with them was strained – too much water under the bridge with no sense of responsibility from either party probably did it.

But here, today, the day after my Little Bear had died, all I wanted was to speak to them. I needed comfort in my utter distress and hoped to get it from them, my own flesh and blood, though looking back now I should have known that it would never come. They'd not given much of a shit about me when I was growing up, so why would that change?

Dad's was the first number I dialled. Not sure why. Was it the number I remembered most clearly in my head? If I were to say I was a smidgen closer to one than the other it was to Mum. Standing in the corridor outside the neonatal ward using the public payphone stuck to the wall was probably not the most private of spaces in the world, but it was all I had. The phone reception at the hospital for mobiles was crap.

Dad answered. All I could say was that Alana had died. He probably spoke and asked a few fretful questions to get his head around what I was saying, but I have no recollection. All I could feel, rushing within me, was an immense, excruciating pain that gradually but frantically soared through my chest, spiking into my whole body, my arms, legs and head. It was the pain of a lifetime of rejection and hurt and a longing for love and care that was now forcing its way out while I talked to the man that had caused some of it.

116

My Alana had been born and now was dead, and I loved her with every bone in my body. In contrast, I had been born and neglected in so many ways, never truly getting my needs met and certainly not emotionally. Love was a foreign concept. I'd suffered mental ill health my entire life, right from when I was a young lad, and today, unbeknown to me, was comeuppance day.

Suddenly, with no plan, only release, I hurled a tyrant of abuse at him down the phone, reeling it off like on a conveyor. It came thick and fast, the force of the verbal vomit coming again and again and again, years of unspoken truths and emotion overflowing and attacking. My Alana was dead and he was gonna get it in barrel loads.

Emotions congealed into one – hurt, pain, anger, sadness, despair, frustration and fury – all mixed together. I knew that as I spoke, saliva spat out in rage. My state of mind did not allow me even to comprehend what was happening on the other end of the line. I couldn't hear what Dad was saying. I was just wanting to speak and shout and accuse.

Even before I was spent, I slammed the phone down, not wanting to listen to myself or him, and not enjoying the feeling of such destructive emotions that allowed the physical pain to rip through me.

'Fuck you!' I screamed, crying through my immense anger. 'Fuck you!'

I needed air. I needed to be able to catch my breath again. I wasn't conscious of anyone that was around me. There could have been people looking on in shock or worry that I might be about to kick off. I have no idea. I walked purposefully towards the door that led to the outside, punching the wall a few times as I went.

'Fuck you!' I repeated.

Breathe, breathe, breathe. I needed to get myself back on a more even keel and find a way of holding it together, but as the minutes passed the same fury raged within me and I wanted to get it out. Thirty-odd years of hurt and pain would take longer than five minutes to die down. I paced a bit, not sure what I was thinking or what I was gonna do next, and then I headed back inside.

Without a thought of what I'd reeled off to my dad ten minutes or so earlier, I found myself back at the payphone. Without hesitation, I rang Mum's number. She was gonna get it too. Before I could say anything, she started to have a go at me.

'Do you know your dad's collapsed after what you did? Do you know what you've done?'

Well, the hurt, pain and fury were completely untamed now. *What I'd done to him? What I'd done to him?*

Fucking hell! What I'd done! What about all the shit that he'd done to me? What about the hundreds of times he'd not been there for me, not showed me that he cared or let me know that I was in anyway important to him? Fuck that! Fuck him!

My brain was whirling at speed. How I stayed on my feet I don't know. Here was Mum, the person most people were able to rely on without question, having a go at me. I wanted her to be my mum, to look after my feelings and show me that she was there for me.

She already knew that Alana had died – she must have heard it first-hand from Dad's end. She couldn't put aside or accept my upset and just sympathise with me about losing my daughter.

No 'So sorry, son, to hear about Alana.'

No 'How sad that she had to die.'

No 'How are you coping, Gary?'

No 'We'll be down with you as soon as we can.'

No 'Tell us where you are, what hospital?'

No 'What about Dana? How is she?'

No 'How's Michelle?'

Why had I thought things would be any different? I'd been rejected for most of my life by them. Why hadn't I learned?

In normal circumstances, I'd never turn to them, knowing that I wasn't ever gonna get what I wanted. It was too late for that. Why had I bothered now? I was furious with myself and with them.

'Fuck you, too!' I snarled.

Here was a woman who, knowing her son had just held his dying child, focused solely on supporting her ex-husband, my dad, the man that she'd shit all over throughout their marriage and eventually walked out on, dragging me with her at the age of twelve, to live with her new man. She'd rather defend him than support me. She had no intention of listening to what I had to say, good or bad. She'd never wanted to listen to what I had to say. It was the end of the line.

118

I slammed down the phone once again, so hurt, so angry and so shattered. I'd spent my lifetime blaming myself for the trouble that I brought to their door, thinking that it was all my fault. The damage was done and festering by the time I was the kid and teenager that was kicking off all the time. They'd done the damage and I'd lived up to it.

At least today had proved to me that everything that they were about didn't include me. My needs weren't what mattered, just theirs. Mum just loved her own needs and loved herself, wanting everything on her terms. I'd wanted her to show *me* love. I wanted her to turn round to me and say, 'I love you, son.'

All those years, I'd still lived in hope that there would be better times ahead, that we'd be able to look forward and make a future where we'd be able to grow out of the shit that was the past and slowly move on. That was never gonna happen now. There was no going back.

My dad has since passed away, a self-reflective man in later life; as for Mum, I have no idea about her, except that she's still breathing. I haven't spoken to her since the day I phoned her from the hospital, and I presume that I won't again.

Wedding Picture – 2000

When I look at this picture, I can see how unwell I was due to my mental health. Back then, I struggled through every day, though I was good at masking it. My clinical psychologist advised us both not to marry; he felt it wouldn't work out. Twenty years on, we have gone through so much together and we still love each other dearly.

Michelle and I in Crete

This was taken in 2002 - our first holiday abroad together. I was three years into my treatment for mental illnesses. Although I had a long way to go, I thought I was turning a corner with my therapy, not knowing that nine months later it was going to take a turn for the very worst.

Scary Doll

This is 'Scary Doll', the teddy that I bought (without thinking!) for Alana when she was in Birmingham's Children's Hospital. I just saw that it was pink! It made us smile when we were in a very dark place. Michelle looks at her every day for she now sits on the dashboard of her car.

18|10|03

L OVE U SHELLY& DANA
DONT WORRY
U look after your end
love u both with all my
heart G<xx Al<xx

My note to Michelle

When I wrote this note I never knew how poignant it would become. Alana was being rushed from the Shrewsbury Royal Hospital to Birmingham Children's Hospital and I had to rush ahead to meet her there, so I wrote a quick note and left it on Michelle's hospital bed. It's the only note I got the chance to write signed from me and Alana and the only one that her mummy would ever receive from her. I honestly believed, at that point, that we would all soon be back together again as a family.

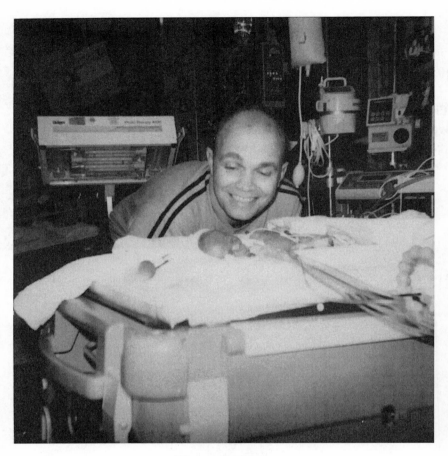

Me and Alana

Looking back at that picture, I honestly believed Alana would make it and wouldn't listen to anyone that doubted that, even the medical professionals. That smile was filled with love for her.

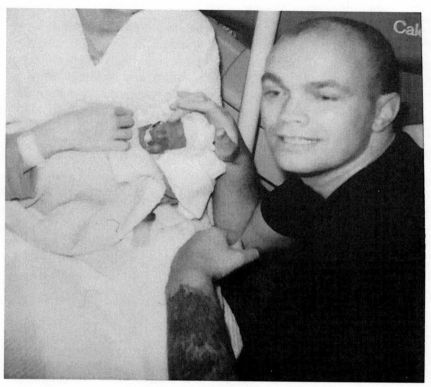

Me and Dana

I still struggle to look at this photo with Dana. It was taken three days
after Alana's death. I just see pain inside myself, the pain of trying to get
my head around what had happened to Alana instead of what it should
have been – celebrating our first cuddle with Dana.

30

Once I'd calmed down a little, I went back to Michelle and Dana. Mick was in and out of the neonatal ward at the time, too, but also wanted to give us the privacy that we needed together. Dana continued to do okay. She was so tiny looking and frail, but she was holding her own with the support of a bit of oxygen just to take the pressure off her having to use all her energy to breath instead of grow.

'I've just rang my mum and dad,' I said to Michelle.

My fury and temper were still bubbling inside, but I covered it well, something that over the years I'd become very good at doing.

'Really?' Michelle looked away from Dana and straight at me in surprise. 'What happened?'

'I told them both what I thought of them. Dad collapsed.'

'What? Is he okay?'

'I'm sure he is. I just couldn't stop myself. I had a right go at Dad, and then when I rang Mum she had a right go at me for having a go at Dad.'

'How did she know?'

'They'd rung her to warn her, so Dad can't be that bad if they were able to do that.'

'What did she say? I'm so sorry, Gary.'

'That's it now,' I told her. 'I don't want anything to do with them again.'

We sat in silence then for a bit, staring at Dana, both knowing that we were mulling over what I'd just done. I had to cut ties, I just had to. It was too painful any other way. Yet the thoughts kept flitting in, wrapped up in guilt.

Look what you've done! It's all your fault. It's your fault for ringing them. You shouldn't have told them what you thought about them. You made him collapse. See, it's always been your fault. No wonder all this has happened to you. It's always your fault.

Then yet more conflicting thoughts would immerge.

Well, they were never there for me, so how is everything my fault? They could have asked about Alana and Dana and Michelle. It wasn't all my fault, surely? Why was I always painted as the bad guy?

I couldn't win.

Still in a despairing mode, but functional, with the embers of what had just taken place still burning inside, Michael and I drove back to Birmingham, leaving Michelle and Dana Bear behind. As much as I tried not to, I couldn't stop thinking about my dad.

Mick didn't have any time for either of my parents either. He'd seen over the years how their neglect of my emotional needs had fucked me up. Nevertheless, I hadn't meant for Dad to collapse, no matter how angry I was with him. However, there was little I could do now, and anyway, I had enough on my plate.

I think I changed my clothes when I got home, but the house was cold and empty and I didn't want to stay there any longer than I needed to. It certainly didn't feel like home. Michael's company kept me moving. I knew that I had to go and register Alana's death and the right time for me was now.

Keep focused, I kept telling myself.

It gave me a purpose of sorts, however distorted. The experience was surreal. I hadn't even been into Shrewsbury to register the Bears' births, and here I was in Birmingham register Alana's death. It was all so wrong. It was all the wrong way round. Children should register their elderly parents' death. Even for adults it's a stressful, sorrowful event.

I just couldn't comprehend the situation I was in. I didn't even know whether they'd let me register Alana's death here before I went to the Shrewsbury office to register the Bears' birth. I hadn't a clue, but it was giving me something to do, so I was gonna try.

People in the street were laughing and joking as we walked towards the registry office. My world might have completely caved in, but elsewhere in other people's world life was moving along. I felt physically sick and sweating profusely with no respite. I'd wipe the sweat from my neck and it was instantly back again. It was the middle of October, so there was no reason to be sweating copious amounts, other than from the stress and anxiety that was surging through me.

Inside, around the reception desk, people held new babies, cooing and swaying them with all the love and care that a parent should. Some were soothing their crying child. As much as I wanted to be them, I also wanted to scream, 'Stop your child from fucking crying,

121

will you? My child is dead!' My hurt and anger were welling below the surface still and it took all the control I had left not to yell out the words.

Then we waited. And waited. Apparently, I could have rung through earlier to say I was coming and have avoided the wait, but who the hell knows that? I didn't. So we waited. They let me register Alana's death. I'm still not sure to this day if they were really meant to, but they did. The process though, was so cold and clinical. I know it has to be. I held Alana's death certificate tightly in my hand. I couldn't contemplate – didn't want to contemplate – a word written on it. I couldn't wait to get out of there to be honest. It was all just too painful.

I also knew that there was another job that I needed to do: go to the undertaker. Fucking funeral directors. I'd never been anywhere near one my whole life and now I was going because my baby daughter was dead. This whole thing was fucked up.

Michelle and I had a brief chat about who we would use and had decided quickly on the one nearest our home. I'd walked past it a thousand times, not noticing it really, but now it was going to play a very important and major part in my life. It was gonna be me who was to organise most of Alana's funeral.

We parked up, Mick still with me. The walk to the undertaker's shopfront was so familiar. In fact, we had to walk past the shop where I'd bought Scary Doll only a few days before. How different things had been then. Alana had been alive and I was excited to be buying her a teddy. I was nervous now. What was I gonna say when I walked in? Would I be able to get the words out? Would they be cold and clinical?

It was surprisingly and eerily quiet when we walked in and shut the door, the noise of the main road outside all but disappearing. A lovely woman met us almost instantly. I could tell that she'd probably been doing this for years; she was well rehearsed and knowledgeable in her field of work. She seemed to ooze care. I tried to explain why I was here, trying to get each sentence out without breaking down, and her patience with me was abundant. We sat in a small, private room, which allowed me to say what I needed to say. It was so, so hard, and the words felt stuck to the back of my throat,

I struggled to get them to leave my mouth, but the lady sat and listened, and gave me time.

The next part was very systematic. There were processes to talk through and arrangements to be made. What I remember most clearly was having to look through a catalogue of coffins. I mean, in what world did anyone want to look through this type of catalogue? It was, though, my job now to pick a coffin for Alana. The little white coffins specifically for babies were so tiny and I picked what I though was most appropriate and fitting for her. It made me feel physically sick. It all felt so wrong.

Costs were discussed in such a caring way; the lady had it off to a tee. She left me and Mick for a moment. Nothing was said for a bit, but then Michael spoke.

'I can pay for all of this, Gary, if you need me to. It's not a problem.'

'No, Mick, it's okay. I need to pay for it myself.'

As kind as his offer was, generous as always, and as much as he was aware that I wasn't flush with money, I knew that I had to pay. I had to pay for my daughter's funeral. There was little more I could do for her now, so it became important for me to do this. Nevertheless, I was so thankful for his offer of support.

The lady returned. We had details to finalise and she said that they'd collect Alana from the Birmingham Children's Hospital and bring her here to their mortuary the following morning. We'd be able to come and pay our last respects to her before her actual funeral. Initially, I wasn't sure how I felt about that, but I yearned to see her nevertheless. I knew for sure that Michelle and her family would want to see her, too.

We walked out and headed straight back to Shrewsbury to Dana and Michelle. It was still surreal to be talking to my wife about the funeral arrangements of our daughter. Michelle seemed to know more about funerals than me. As Alana was going to be buried in the traditional Catholic way, she was able to fill in the gaps about the service and what needed to be arranged. She said she'd write the prayers that others were going to say. I had no idea how she could get her head around doing that, but she wanted to write them. Mick and I stayed in Michelle's room for a while, but it felt stifled with grief. Some of her family were there, too, and no one really knew what to talk about. I decided that me and Mick would go home, back to Birmingham, to be on the move again, so we had something to do other than sit and focus on how awful we all felt.

We called in to see Dana on our way out. Seeing her lying there, I so wanted her to grow, get bigger, feed better, breath without any oxygen to support her – all the things that would be signs to me that she was going to be ok. My head was so full of what had happened to Alana that I was scared to think about Dana too much. It scared me to love her, even though I did, so much.

The following morning, I knew Alana would have been brought to the funeral home and that I could see her. Michelle was still in Shrewsbury so for now, it was just gonna be Mick and I. What was I expecting? I didn't know. How was I going to react? I hadn't a clue. Mick was leaving to go home straight after, having to go home because of work commitments.

My heart was beating so hard in my chest when I got there that I thought everyone would be able to hear it if they came near. I walked into the room where she was laid out. All that was to the right of me was a tiny white coffin with no lid. I knew that Alana was lying there, but almost didn't want to walk over and look inside. Everything was so silent.

Just walk over, I told myself.

And there she was, still wearing the beautiful baby outfit that we'd dressed her in at the Children's Hospital. As before, she looked like she was sleeping. I wished she was. She looked like my beautiful baby girl, my little Alana Bear, and I wanted to pick her up, out of the coffin, and hold her. I bend down gently and kissed her on her head.

'I'll never stop loving you, Alana.'

I spoke to her in my head, telling her that I'd love her forever and never forget her, that I'd make sure Dana knew all about her and that we'd include her in everything, even though she was gone. Alana would live on through her identical sister, Dana. In that moment, I knew that how important it was to be a good dad to Dana, that this was my chance to turn the tide and do good all-round.

It was Michael's partner Fiona who had gifted the girls' blankets, each with her name on, so it only seemed fitting that Alana have her blanket in with her to keep her warm. It's crazy how the mind finds comfort in such small things.

I wanted to stay and sit with her for the day and not leave her, like I'd not wanted to leave her when we were sitting in the Children's Hospital. I knew that this was going to be one of the last times that I'd get to see her. I knew I was coming back with Michelle to see her one last time, just before her funeral, but it was still hard to drag myself away. I was her dad. It angered me that I couldn't change places with her. By being here and still being able to see her, she wasn't quite gone to me. How could I leave her on her own again? She needed me. In reality, it was me who needed her.

31

Dana was now almost a week old when the nurse said that she was well enough for us to have our first hold.

Holy shit! She was so tiny, so delicate and so fragile. I didn't want to break her. Inside, my head was screaming: *You can't do it! You can't do it!*

They handed Dana to Michelle. Dana was still covered in wires and oxygen tubes, but she was in Michelle's arms, and it was a moment I will never forget. At last, Michelle was able to touch her in real life. We were able to hold her, and not just through the plastic of the incubator.

I knelt down next to them and held Dana's head. The relief and quiet joy on Michelle's face was mirrored in mine. This was my little girl – my other little girl. I was able to stroke her skin, talk to her and give her a kiss on her head while she sat for the first time, snug and content, on her mummy's lap. Michelle smiled down at our bundle of joy, a real smile. It was heart-breaking and touching at the same time.

This was surely the start of how it was meant to be. This was what we'd been waiting for, how the picture should have played out. The moment was beautiful, but almost lost in the stress and tension that could not just be switched off.

After what must have only been less than a minute or two, the nurse said it was best that Dana return to her incubator – her 'home'. My God, she was so small – not even near 2lb in weight – yet so perfect in every way. I couldn't help stare. When she moved, even the slightest movement of her head or finger, it made us sit up and take notice.

'Look, she just moved her finger!'

'There she goes again. She just moved her head a bit!'

Everything and anything that showed that she was living, breathing, fighting and with us was absorbed with awe. I must admit though, that I was – in all honesty – glad to see her settled back in her incubator. It was where she needed to be. As much as I wanted her to be strong and well, and doing all the things that 'normal' babies do, I knew that for now, her need was to be in the incubator with other people looking after her.

It frightened me to think that I'd have to be 'in charge' of Dana at some point in the future, and would have to care for her once she was strong enough and allowed to come home. The people around me seemed so at ease moving Dana around like she was huge, not tiny! I know that this was their day job and I had no experience whatsoever of dealing with such a tiny being, but I was in awe of them. I felt so incompetent in comparison, not that they ever made me feel like that.

Meanwhile, everything about being around Dana was still filled with fear and excruciating uncertainty for me. I didn't want to trust that she was going to get stronger and come back to Birmingham with us; I didn't want to give her my heart.

It sounds selfish and I guess, from my point of view, it was. It was already broken and I didn't know how much more it could handle. I knew Dana needed her daddy. I knew I had to be strong for her, strong for Michelle and strong for myself, but to be that for everyone meant that I needed to keep it all in, keep my emotions in check and 'be a man', like my dad had once told me to be when I'd asked for his help. 'Be a man.'

That was who I was, and that's how I'd act.

32

The days moved in and out of each other as a confusing and debilitating waiting game.

Waiting for Alana's funeral.

Waiting to hear, every hour, if Dana was still doing well, upping her milk consumption by only millimetres, and waiting to see if her gut would be able to take the increase, lessening the amount of oxygen she needed, and waiting to see if she'd need more again.

Waiting, grieving and shitting myself.

Meantime, the funeral director informed us that, if we wanted to, we could go and see Alana in the chapel of rest the day before she was brought into church, ahead of her funeral. Because of Michelle's religious customs, Alana was to be brought into church the night before her actual funeral. I didn't understand what it was all about, why this was or why people put themselves through two days of a 'funeral experience', so to speak, but it was Michelle's tradition, so I went with it.

I'd never been to a funeral like this before. Up where I come from, when someone dies, funerals are just one day: church, cemetery, wake-celebration with food and booze. They're quick, too. As soon as you're dead you're practically buried – from death to burial was about two to three days normally. How different this would be.

How many funerals had I been to and not really thought too hard and long about the grief of the family involved? Plenty. Yeah, you think about them on that day, but then life takes over and you go about your own business. This time, it was me. I was the one grieving and I didn't want anyone to take it for granted. We'd organise food and a gathering for after the cemetery, but they'd be no celebrating Alana's life, and definitely no booze. It just wasn't right.

Anyway, Michelle said that Alana would be left in church overnight. In her faith, it's something to do with being 'in the presence of God', I think. I didn't get this. Wasn't she going to be with God forever now, anyway?

The main reason really, bar tradition, was that having a short service the evening before her actual funeral, called 'the reception into the church', gave people the opportunity to come and pay their respects, especially those who weren't able to take time away from work and their own lives on a weekday morning, but who had been praying for us and asking after all of us for many, many months throughout the pregnancy – they were able to come, come after work, or whatever.

So it was that morning, the morning before Alana was taken to the church that I would get to see her again for the very last time: our last day together. Did I want to see her? Yes, of course I did. It ached to think about not seeing her.

Michael had driven down again, with Fiona this time, to be with me for the funeral. He'd been in constant touch since returning home, but knew that the next few days were gonna be tough on me, so he was here again. Him being around gave me a sense of comfort in the madness, a familiarity.

He said he'd come with me to see Alana. I was gonna go back to Shrewsbury straight after, to take Michelle home so that she could also see Alana before the funeral, too. Here we were again, visiting my Little Bear. It was just as hard to leave her this time as every time, but I had no choice. I had to walk away. Anyway, Michelle was coming home, and I had to go and collect her from Shrewsbury. I wished that she was coming home for good and bringing Dana with her, but that was too much to ask for. She was coming home for just one night, and for no other reason than to bury her daughter.

After I arrived back in Shrewsbury and helped Michelle get herself together to go home, the nursing staff asked if we'd like to have another hold of Dana before we left. The staff must have been so aware of how heartbroken we were. We were on our way to bury our child. Getting another opportunity to hold Dana was probably keeping Michelle sane.

I sat and looked on, holding Dana's little hands, but never in a million years did I want to actually hold her at this point. She was so tiny and fragile looking and my large, cumbersome hands didn't have a 'go gentle' function, so I didn't want to risk it.

Watching Dana and Michelle together filled moments with awe and all-consuming love, but they would be whisked away and consumed with the grief and reality of what we were living. The anxiety and heartbreak that we were carrying between the two of us was palpable.

We drove home – well, almost. Before arriving back, we went to the chapel of rest to see Alana together. Michelle was tearful before we even got there, understandably so. Seeing Alana lying there again, still the same, brought more certainly that this was the end. We put some rosary beads in with her and a photograph of Dana.

We stayed with her for a while, but I knew that this was the very last time that I'd see her face, touch her cold skin, and be able to kiss her and tell her, face to face, that I loved her. Later that day, the small, white lid would be placed on top of her coffin and she'd be truly gone from me forever.

It was time to go, another room to have to walk out of another place to leave her behind. It had been excruciatingly difficult to do it at the hospital and at every visit here, but now it was on a different level. This was it.

As before, I just wanted to take her home with me and keep her safe. If I'd had the choice, I'd have carried her out of the undertaker's and buried her in my garden, just so that I could keep her close. My emotions were crushing my insides now.

Fortunately for the both of us, the drive to our house was going to be short, less than a mile; but walking back to the car, hearing the hustle and bustle of the traffic and the people walking about, living their everyday lives so normally, made my senses flood with every sound and smell. How was I going to get my legs to walk to the car, sit in it and turn the key? The nearer I got, the more the emotion rose, emotions so strong that the tipping point was near. I wanted to yell out to the world, 'My daughter's in there. My dead daughter's in there! I've just had to leave her. She's only a baby.'

The short journey was quiet, but the emotions were loud. As I pulled into the road leading to our house, I was abruptly stopped by a delivery truck dropping rolls of neatly folded lawn to a house not far from mine. It was blocking the road so that no car could get passed and they weren't the slightest bit bothered that they were making me wait. My frustration grew quickly. Just an acknowledgement would have done, a 'won't be long – sorry to keep you waiting' gesture, would have been enough. To me, ignoring me was just rude.

'Are they taking the fucking piss? They've not even made any attempt to say sorry for keep me waiting or anything!' I screamed at the windscreen. My temper rising at speed.

'Give them a minute,' Michelle said. I know now that she felt my temper rising, too, but I wasn't aware then.

One of the guys looked directly at me and still didn't acknowledge me. Well, that was it, that was the red rag to the bull that was waiting to explode. I jumped out of the car and let rip, with nothing rational left inside.

'Are you taking the fucking piss, mate?' I yelled and went straight into the man's face. 'What the fuck do you think you're doing? There's no need for you to park in the middle of the road and you're just taking the piss expecting everyone to wait for you!' My temper was out of control.

The man, appearing up for it for the first few seconds, must have known I was a man with his temper let loose. 'All right man, calm down, calm down. We'll be done in a minute.'

'Calm down? You haven't even got the fucking decency to acknowledge that we're waiting, you fucking cunt!' I continued to yell. How I didn't hit him there and then, I have no idea.

From behind me, I could hear Michelle crying, screaming at me to get back in the car, trying to balance herself on the car bonnet, still unable to walk freely. 'Stop it, Gary. Stop, Gary. Don't do this... We've got a dead daughter! We've got a dead daughter!'

Her cries of desperation, despair and anguish fell on deaf ears. I turned to face her. She was balancing herself on the car, holding her stomach and crying hysterically. Still nothing rational came to mind, just anger. How dare she interfere!

'Get back in the fucking car.' My anger was being directed in all directions. 'And you,' I pointed to the driver, 'move the fucking truck, now!'

With that I got back in the car, and drove the short distance to home – only about 200 metres – with me fucking and bollocking them and Michelle all the way. Fury raged inside me, while tears of hurt and embarrassment poured from Michelle.

It wasn't until I walked into the house that I'd realised what I'd done. The anger was now beginning to subside and gave way to the reality and guilt of the scene I'd just caused. Fucking hell! What had just happened? Michelle was sobbing uncontrollably. It shouldn't have been like this. This was the first time she'd been home in almost two weeks. I'd wanted to make it special for her – or as special as it could be under all the circumstances –but I'd ruined it. I'd ruined it because of my fucking awful temper that had erupted as swiftly as time itself. She didn't deserve that. She was the mother of the Bears, she'd just seen her dead daughter for the first time since the night that she died, and there she was, trying to calm me down – and not forgetting she could still hardly fucking walk.

And what about those poor men? They weren't deserving of my wrath.

'What you did was wrong, Gary, so wrong. Nothing justifies that!'

'Fucking hell! I need to go up and apologise! What the fuck!'

With that, I left Michelle and walked around the corner to the two men, still unloading the rolls of lawn but not blocking the roadway anymore. I could tell as I approached them that they were fearful of me, of what I might do to them and of what I might say. I spoke as I walked towards them.

'Listen, mate, I'm so sorry. I've got no excuse for what I just done.' I held my hands up apologetically.

They'd obviously heard Michelle say that we'd lost our daughter and they both came and shook my hand. 'So sorry, mate, to hear about your loss. We understand.'

They couldn't have been nicer, these guys who had just got an almighty bollocking from me. I was so wrong to do that. They certainly didn't deserve it in any way. How easy, though, it had been for me to go from 0 to 10. Typical behaviour of old – no rationality.

Michelle was waiting nervously when I arrived back. I could tell from her expression that she'd feared that they'd be 'round two'. She hadn't deserved it either, and I made sure that she knew that.

33

Before I knew it, I was tightening my black tie around my neck, getting ready to take Alana into church. We were meeting the undertaker there, with Alana held in the back of one of their black cars by a member of their staff.

How can anyone prepare for these moments? How does anyone know what to do? My good mates Jimmy and Glen arrived from London in time for the church in the evening. Others were travelling down in the morning. There was already a crowd gathering outside the church when we arrived. Most people couldn't make eye contact with us. I probably couldn't with them either, but I could feel the stares of them all. Many people Michelle knew came to shake my hand and offer condolences, but I felt like a fish out of water.

In the darkness of that November afternoon, Alana arrived. I leaned in and took her tiny, white coffin from the pall-bearer and turned to face the crowd. I saw nothing. This was my duty, my 'daddy' duty, to carry my daughter into church. My focus was pinpoint sharp – it needed to be. I was going to carry my daughter into church, the most important job I'd ever had. This was all that I could do for Alana now, hold her tight and keep her safe.

I walked solo down the aisle, knowing Michelle would be following, but needing to think only of Alana, and I placed her gently on the table at the front of the aisle among the yellow rose petals. It was the longest walk of my life and yet I wanted to drag my heels so I could keep her with me for longer. I didn't want to let her go. I remember my mate Basher saying much later on that he was worried I might drop her. No way. I didn't even want Alana to be a foot away from me, but I was led into the front seat, as is tradition.

What was said and prayed for is now a blur. There is no money on God's earth that would help me to remember, although I have a vague memory of the priest coming down from the altar to shake my hand. This was a handshake of sympathy; it couldn't be a handshake of anything else because this whole fucking thing was so wrong. I wasn't meant to be burying my daughter tomorrow! The world had become a massive, fucked-up place.

Once the priest had done what he needed to, people came to the front to sympathise. There were so many. I shook so many hands and thanked people for coming. Many faces were familiar – people I'd met since moving to Birmingham – but more weren't, and the generosity and sincerity of their words and their sympathies were real.

Many of those there were Michelle's family and friends. Many were of her parent's generation and had known her most of her life. I was the near-stranger amongst them tonight. Sure, I knew people, but I'd only been in Birmingham for three years compared, to Michelle's near lifetime. Michael and Fiona were with me, as always, so loyal and dependable. Jimmy and Glen were there, and my treasured mates from home were travelling down after work to be here with me later and for the morning. They were all making such an effort to come and support me. It meant the world to me and still chokes me today when I think about what they all mean to me, each and every one of them.

I had no family here of my own. No mum, no dad, no brother. No one. Why? Why me again? Why was coming to their granddaughter's/niece's funeral so far removed from their priorities when all of these other people – mostly strangers to me – were here shaking my hand and giving me support?

Did I really want my family to come, though? After all, my relationship with all of them on all levels was poor. That said, could I have handled them being here? Probably not. What would I have done with them if they'd come? What words could make up for the lifetime of missed opportunities and lost time?

Yes, I knew Dad's health wasn't great, but he managed to go to far-off places for holidays. I knew some family members worked and would have had to take time off, but then so did everyone else. I knew it was a long way to come, but my friends were gonna manage it. All of the points that I tried to justify out of long-term habit were now unjustifiable. They should have been here, seeing what I was seeing and touching what I was touching – Alana's tiny coffin – taking the palm of my hand in a hand shake.

The tightness of the emotion sitting inside my chest was still excruciating. Here I was, leaving Alana alone yet again in the church overnight. Michelle reassured me that she'd be safe and in the presence of holiness, but it didn't help. I still had to leave her all over again. How many times was that now? And it would happen all over again tomorrow. Reflecting now, I'd always seen churches as quiet places, places of sanctuary and of peace. Maybe I should have spent a bit more time in them, too.

I wanted people to leave now, not out of disrespect, but out of the need to breathe easier. Deep breaths weren't near deep enough to fill me with the oxygen I needed.

A few of us went to the local pub on the way home, because my mates had arrived from home after their long journey. This was an odd one. It was something that always happened at home when I was growing up and most of us really needed a drink. Michelle went home and it wasn't long before I followed on. It didn't feel right to be in that happy, social place when my sadness was so great.

Michelle's parents had kindly offered rooms for the night for my friends, moving out themselves to accommodate them. Michael and Fiona stayed with us. Michelle rang the hospital straight after the service, and thankfully Dana was still doing okay. There were no real changes, which allowed the two of us to spend a night huddled together in our own, familiar bed.

The darkness seeped between us, but sleep didn't come. Michelle still kept her glasses on and had a light close. Being on high alert continued.

34

Morning arrived, signalling the start of the day we were going to bury our beautiful Little Bear, Alana. A hard day ahead. A horrible day ahead. The funeral of a child is one that no parent should ever have to live through.

The hospital reported that Dana had had a good night, so we knew we'd be okay to attend Alana's funeral. Had Dana taken any slight turn for the worst, me and Michelle had agreed that she'd be driven back to Shrewsbury, and I'd bury Alana without her. What a dilemma: bury your child or go and be with one who might die because they're poorly, too? There were going to be no winners here, but thankfully Dana was doing okay.

Living in a blur, before we knew it the two of us were back outside the church again, surrounded by people who wanted to support us. I was greeted by my friends from home – some I'd know all of my life, others not for quite so long, but all very important to me. My heart swelled with pride at how genuine their care and thoughts for the two of us were.

At that moment, I needed these people more than I'd ever needed them before. With years of camaraderie between us, through happy, sad and tough times, we'd always stuck together and shared what needed to be shared. Every single one of them was as significant to me as the next, and I will take their kindness to my own grave.

Today I was burying my daughter, who, sadly, they hadn't had the chance to meet, but they would be here by my side. Everything about them was familiar and comforting in an atmosphere of such sorrow. I knew I'd be okay. They gave me a dose of much-needed courage. I knew with them there, I'd be able to get through the day. Neither my mum nor my dad showed up. I hadn't expected them to.

Inside, we walked towards Alana's coffin, still in the middle of the aisle where we'd left her the previous evening. Strangely, it looked even smaller now. I couldn't help thinking it didn't feel right that she'd spent the night here. After all, babies weren't meant to be left alone.

That walk to the top of the church seemed never-ending, but I wanted it to be long and drawn out. I wanted it to last for as long as was possible. The longer I could drag my heels, the longer I could have Alana near me. I didn't want to bury her. I wanted to keep her. My Little Bear.

The service started and continued without my interaction. I stood and sat when I saw others doing it. Hymns were sung, readings said and blessings given. I noticed that Father Paul, the chaplain from Shrewsbury Hospital, came to the service, too – a very touching gesture of support that meant a lot to me. He'd not only met Alana, but also baptised her. There were very few people that had had the opportunity to meet Alana and he was one of them.

Meanwhile, me and Michelle held hands, knowing that soon, very soon, Alana would be lowered into the ground. At the final hymn, it was time to lift Alana again and carry her down the church and out to the funeral car. As I held her little white coffin as tightly as I could, the pressure of the grief inside my lungs was immense, but my attention had to be solely focused on protecting Alana.

I dared to look up only once, to be met with fleeting glances. Most people looked away, their eyes darting in another direction, the sight of such a scene too much to bear. I understood. But I was oblivious to what was going on all around me. As Alana's dad, I was going to be the one to take her to her final resting place, even if it killed me inside to do so. I was proud to do that.

Was it right for me to feel so proud in all of this sorrow? Was it? But I did. I felt so proud to be her dad and so proud that this was what I got to do, no one else, just me. Just me and my little girl.

We sat in silence again in the funeral car. I'd got in holding Alana so tightly and still had my arms around her coffin, now resting on my knee. I was so afraid of moving her unnecessarily.

'Am I holding her right?' I asked Michelle. 'I don't know what I'm meant to do. I've never had to hold a coffin on my knee before.' My body felt numb. I needed to know I was doing ok.

'You're doing just right, hon,' and Michelle placed her hand on the side of Alana's coffin, too.

They often say that in the saddest of moments, humour rises its joyful head and makes you smile. Well, we had one of those moments in the back of the car. As we sat there, waiting for what we thought was a lifetime while everyone else got to their cars and prepared to follow us to the cemetery, the priest arrived at the door and jumped in the front part of our funeral car. We had no idea that he was going to come with us.

'You don't mind, do you?' he asked. 'It's easier for me to jump in with you and get to the cemetery ahead of everyone. Otherwise you'll be waiting for me to get there and park.'

To say the least, I was a bit taken aback – and a bit pissed off, if I'm honest – but it was such a shock that in such circumstances, I just went along with it. Well, you do, don't you? Anyway, what could I have said? Get out and make your own way there? Hardly! So, our quiet time with Alana had been rudely interrupted.

Me and Michelle just looked at each other and held back an awkward grin. A fucking cheek, was what I actually thought. Someone could have warned us! We didn't chat after that. Our private time had been intruded upon, and our words were left hanging in the air now that we had extra company.

The cemetery was only a ten minute drive away. Again, I wanted the time to drag. For once, I'd have been happy to have been stuck in a traffic jam.

Please God, let the journey go slowly, I prayed, silently.

I wanted Alana to stay on my knee for as long as possible; she'd never climb up on my knee as a little girl now. Reality struck hard. This was gonna be it, this was gonna be the end of the road.

Just ten minutes later we were driving through the large iron gates of the cemetery. What immediately registered with me were the hundreds and hundreds of graves, stretching out forever. We spotted the children's section immediately as we drove round. You could spot it a mile away: the many bright colours, and lots of toys and teddy bears propped up on graves , each with its own story to tell.

I noticed that those cars in the convoy behind us were now also parked up, and people were walking towards the graveside. Some were already waiting, having arrived at the cemetery before we did, many holding each other for support, others with their heads bowed, but all dealing with it in their own way.

The undertaker led me to the grave, me still carrying Alana in my arms. Holding her precious body as tenderly and respectfully as I could, I still did not know whether I was doing it right. The crowds continued to gather. I could hear the slamming of car doors, the clatter of heels and then silence. I never once look up; I couldn't. I daren't. The welling up emotion was huge, more than I'd ever felt before. Tears poured and I didn't stop them.

Now I was finally going to have to let Alana go for the last time. There'd be no next time, no time after that, no one more chance. This was it. My core was truly broken. I'd been told by the undertaker that they'd have to place Alana in the grave, but I wanted to do it. I wanted to do it more than anything. More prayers were said by the priest, and then it was the moment I dreaded.

My chest felt tight and heavy, and I could feel pain creeping into my arms, back and neck. I felt sick inside. Now it was time to let Alana go, time to say a final goodbye. I placed her at the opening to the grave, and the pallbearers lowered her down, lowering my heart as they did so.

Heartbreak.

This was her resting place now. It took every ounce of willpower and respect in me to not lean over, reach in and dig her back out.

As is tradition, we were handed soil to throw on the coffin. I wanted to do it because it was the thing to do, but I didn't want to be the one who started filling in her grave either. The sound of the soil hitting her coffin went through me.

Please do it gently, please do it gently, I thought, as the soil fell. *Don't crush her.*

Holding Michelle's hand, we just stared and stared at the grave, the reality of what we had been through – and were going through – hitting us hard. It crossed my mind that there should be a law against burying children like this, alone and helpless. You'd never leave them alone if they were alive. They needed to be close to their family, surely. She should have come home with us and I'd have buried her safely in the garden.

I hoped beyond hope that there was a better place where Alana's spirit had gone to, and that she was now playing freely, and having fun – but I wasn't sure I could trust that hope.

35

We left the graveside first and so were the first back at the parish centre. My insides were like a turmoil of wires, like a satnav programmed in the wrong direction. Nothing made sense. Very soon, I was surrounded by people who were again offering condolences but I didn't want to be here. I didn't quite know where I wanted to be in fact, but certainly not here.

I stayed close to my friends. That was comfort enough for me, for now. Funeral normality was happening all around. People ate plates of sandwiches, chicken legs and coleslaw. Eat? There was no way I could do that. Cups of tea and coffee were served; we'd decided it would be too disrespectful to have the bar open. It was a child's funeral. I didn't want anyone having a laugh at the bar and getting pissed. I'd probably end up lamping them one, if I wasn't careful, if I thought they weren't being respectful enough to Alana. I didn't need any more emotional hikes.

When we needed to, me and Michelle walked around the room and thanked people for coming. It was so hard to do. Everyone was genuine, of course, but it felt like I had the strongest theatre spotlight beaming down on me from above, the unwanted star of the show. I knew I had no way of turning it off, but it made me feel vulnerable amongst others.

By mid-afternoon, people started to say their goodbyes and begin their journey home, but there was no going home for me and Michelle. We still had Dana on our minds every second, so we knew that we'd be heading straight back to Shrewsbury to be with her. Michelle had been in contact with the nurses in Shrewsbury throughout the day. Dana was still stable and that was such a relief.

My friends from home had the longest journey and headed off. Saying goodbye was not easy. None of us are natural huggers at the best of times, certainly not to each other, but today was the exception. I hugged each and every one of the sincerely. It had meant the world to me that they were there. I was so sad to see them drive off the car park. However, Michael and his partner Fiona were going to drive to Shrewsbury first, to visit Dana, before heading back to Berwick. This would be quite some detour on an already long journey – such support from home.

It was a relief to get back to Dana, and catch up with what had been happening with her in detail. I hadn't seen her for a whole day, but little had changed. She was doing okay. Just okay, but that was better than not okay.

Michael and Fiona stayed with us for a little while, but we were all conscious of the long journey that was ahead of them, and eventually I had another sad goodbye to say. I was gutted to see Mick leave, my big mate with a big heart. I could feel the instant loneliness creeping back in as I waved his car off into the darkness of the October night.

I stood outside for a long time, lost in my own thoughts – and not good ones. I'd struggled with my mental health my whole life, plagued by emotional neglect, multiple traumas, attachment issues, anxiety, depression and more. It felt like my life was a constant battle, and I was sinking deeper and darker, no matter how much I tried to resist it. Already four years into treatment for my 'issues', receiving psychotherapy twice weekly, it would take a different slant again now, wouldn't it? I hadn't foreseen having to deal with severe bereavement, as well as everything else.

Like I've said, I thought I'd been to hell and back with my emotions many times, but this was something off the scale. Standing there in the cold, I couldn't envisage what any type of normal life might look like. What would it resemble now? I folded my arms across myself. I was just like the little lost boy of old, not knowing what to do in a world that made no sense. I wanted to fix everything, make it all right but in reality I couldn't fix myself, let alone anything else.

Picture a prisoner trapped in a cell: that was how my head felt. No matter how many internal walls and doors I knock on to get out or how many times I cry out loud, there is no escape. The cell still remains the cell and I am its prisoner.

How easy it would have been at this point to go back to the destructive comfort of my old ways, anything to ease the pain. Alcohol had been both friend and foe over many years and the temptation to just have a few too many to drown out the pain, and the blame, was strong. However, as strong as it was, I knew it wouldn't be an option. I'd already lost Alana, and if I started

141

hammering drink into me now, I knew I'd lose Dana and Michelle as well.

That brought a real sense of fear, too. I don't think I'd cope with any more loss. The anger was always in the background, ready to pounce when provoked and I could even feel it stir again at the thought of even considering alcohol again.

My thoughts were interrupted, and reality kicked back in, as two nurses walked past me on their way out of the hospital. I watched them as they walked on, away from me, then I turned and made my way slowly back inside, and headed to the neonatal ICU where Michelle was sitting with Dana.

The staff, obviously knowing the hardship of the day, asked if we would like to hold Dana again, out of the incubator. This was a wow moment in such gloom. Two days running we got to take her out of her incubator! It was amazing how just having Dana nearer, feeling her next to us was amazing, even though it was only a foot nearer than when she was in the incubator.

I still didn't feel confident enough to hold her myself, but I know that Michelle couldn't get over her weightlessness. The nurses said that babies calm as soon as they were with their mothers and it was the same the other way round. As nervous and distressed as we both were, having Dana out of her incubator was calming to us, too.

A beginning of how it was meant to be, a feeling of how it was going to be when she grew and got a bit stronger and a bit heavier. Hope lay in front of us and it was a gorgeous glimpse of hope.

36

The day before the funeral, as if there wasn't enough going on, Michelle was also moved out of her room off the ward. She couldn't just stay there indefinitely.

'I can't leave Dana.' Michelle said. 'I can't go back home.' The thought just wasn't possible. 'I need to stay in Shrewsbury.'

We were preparing for her to go and stay in a bed-and-breakfast or somewhere – there was no way she could be able to be as far away as Birmingham. As chance would have it, the neonatal ward had just finished one of two parents' rooms within the confines of the neonatal ward, and offered one to her. She jumped at the chance.

Thankfully, not only did she now not have to face the upheaval of finding somewhere to stay and then have the hassle of getting back and forth from the hospital every day, but also she was now even closer to Dana – a corridor length, granted, but still nearer. She was delighted. It had been a while since I'd been allowed to stay, but on this night, the night of Alana's funeral, they let us spend it together. The light stayed on, as did Michelle's glasses.

Now that the funeral was over, for me there was a lull, not in terms of anxiety – both of us were still very much on daily high alert with Dana, always suspecting that things would change – but in terms of, *what do I do now?* I needed to keep busy and distracted. Now there was no funeral to organise and occupy me, there were no people to see or places to be. It felt functionless, and for me that wasn't helpful.

I needed to keep myself busy just to occupy my mind away from Michelle, Dana and Alana. I didn't want to have to think about how reality really was. I knew how traumatic and shitty it was and I didn't want to be constantly reminded. It hurt too much. And yet, I continued once, often twice, daily trips back and forth to Shrewsbury to spend time with Michelle and Dana Bear.

Michelle would sit with Dana all day. Some days and hours were a little more relaxed than others, but the beeps around Dana continued night and day. It was so easy to lose track of time. Doctors and nurses changed shifts and went back and forth between home and work, but Michelle stayed put. At least the change of shift brought new, yet now familiar faces, and reminded us that time had moved, rather than stood still.

I'd drive from Birmingham every morning and arrive about lunchtime. Staff would make us leave the neonatal ward to eat – it was easy to forget. Michelle's family and friends were so committed to supporting us too, and they would often call in to Shrewsbury – not that you can call in to Shrewsbury from Birmingham. It's a 100+ mile round trip, but they still came, often laden with snacks and goodies for us.

They didn't even always get to see Dana. They'd come and sit in the waiting area of the maternity unit and we'd come out to them. A change of face and conversation was always welcome, but at the same time difficult. Conversations rightly still focused on Dana, Alana's death and what might happen next. For me, it was sometimes difficult to leave Dana, especially when my anxiety was high. Other times, I just wasn't in the frame of mind to come out and make small-talk. Nevertheless, they never stopped coming to support us.

As Dana looked to becoming more stable, and when there was little change in her wellbeing other than small, forward changes on a daily basis, myself and Michelle would occasionally venture on a short walk to the local corner shop, just around the corner from the maternity ward. We did it simply to get out, see the outside world again, get a perspective on the real life going on around us, and for a bit of variety, too.

It's strange the things you notice. Beside others just going about their normal life, it was the change in the weather that really got me. It'd seemed to have gone from autumn to winter in a day. It wasn't a day, of course, but my life felt like one long day at the moment. Winter really was kicking in, though. I could see it in the nakedness of the trees and I could feel it in the temperature of the breeze and the need for a jacket of some sort. I felt like I'd bypassed autumn completely because of the events of the past few weeks. October had come and gone and we were now well into November.

Outside and within me, winter was definitely setting in.

37

One day we were sitting with Dana, and the winter sun, low in the sky, was blazing through the window of the neonatal ward. The blinds were up and the slight warmth was welcome. I happened to be chatting to the staff, unaware that I was moving back and forth on my stool as I spoke.

'Hey, hey! Watch!' Michelle gasped in elation.

'What? What am I meant to be looking at?'

'Look, it just happened again!'

'What?' I was laughing now at what I couldn't see!

'See? When you move on your stool, Dana shuts her eyes!'

'What? How?'

'Do it again, do it again!'

So I moved to the side again, and sure enough, Dana's eyes closed! As soon as I moved back again to shade the sunlight, she'd open her eyes again. I couldn't believe it! She was opening and closing her eyes on my movements!

'Look! Look! I'm doing it, I'm doing it!'

We laughed and laughed and laughed. I got the staff to look, too. I was so excited. I couldn't stop myself from doing it over and over again. I wanted to keep doing it and making Dana open and close her eyes – open when I blocked the sun, closed when I let the sun through.

Like any baby, there are such small, significant moments that mean the world, and this was my first real interaction with Dana. Sure, I'd held her hand and stroked her head and kissed her, but this was something that we were both part of. Me and Dana. Daddy and daughter, Daddy Bear and Little Bear. I will always cherish what happened in those short moments. For me, it was the first time I got to play with Dana. Me and Dana, playing in the sun.

Gradually, Dana began to feed a little more. Although Michelle's milk was never in any way substantial, she never gave up trying to express it, and slowly, daily, Dana's weight increased an ounce at a time. Because she was now much more stable, the nurses contacted hospitals in Birmingham with a view to her being moved nearer to home. We knew that she wouldn't be able to come 'home home' just yet, but it'd mean that Michelle could move back home, too, and life wouldn't be journeying back and forth to Shrewsbury for me either.

Every day they tried for us, and every day drew a blank. Then one Monday, early afternoon, on my drive to Shrewsbury, Michelle called me on my mobile.

'They've got a place! They've got an intensive care cot free in Birmingham City Hospital! We're coming home!' she shrieked, with great excitement.

This news was exactly what I needed. A swell of happiness rose within me. They were coming home! They were finally coming home! Dana would just be six miles up the road instead of sixty. We'd be able to go in and be with her every day, but to come home as a couple and be at home.

Home had turned into a very lonely place over the past month. It was just me, walking around its empty space, trying to fill time and wait for the next day to come. I'm not sure I was even bothered enough to keep fresh milk in the fridge or bread in the cupboard. Life had become about the journey to and from Shrewsbury, once or twice a day. I'd only use one cup, plate, knife and fork. I didn't need more.

It took me back to years gone by, when I lived in London for a bit. I was on my own then, too, for much of the time and would empty my can of Big Soup into the saucepan to heat it up, scoff that down with a load of bread, give it a quick swill out and empty a tin of rice pudding into the same pan. Saved on washing up! And here I was again, home alone with one plate, pan and cup.

I didn't want to be at home, especially on my own. It left me with my thoughts for too long. This home used to have Michelle in it, and we were so hopeful that we'd have our two Bears here one day. I'd lost one Bear, and I was praying for the other, and frankly, I wanted to drink alcohol to numb the thoughts and feelings that my body was carrying.

I hadn't drank for years, but I knew the effect. I just wanted to feel something else, maybe sleep a little. I remember seeing bottles of wine in the house and an opened bottle of vodka. Wine wasn't my thing, but I had to take the bottle of vodka and pour it down the sink in case the temptation to float into oblivion got too much.

146

Occasionally, there'd be a knock at the front door, but I never went to it. I didn't want to open it. I didn't want to talk to anyone, and I certainly didn't want anyone to ask me how I was. I didn't want to have to tell them about anything. I didn't want to have to relive anything. I spent a lot of time in the bedroom just sitting and lying in my destructive thoughts – all negative, all self-sabotaging, all blaming and full of guilt.

Did I fight for Alana enough? Did they do something wrong? Could I have done something differently that would have made her live?

The thoughts were crucifying. Then on a different tangent, I wondered whether I should be preparing the house for Michelle coming home, and painting a room for Dana when she got home. Wasn't that what Dads did? Got the baby room ready?

We hadn't done anything towards preparing for the Bears while Michelle was pregnant, because it seemed like we were tempting fate. Should I be doing something now ready for Dana when she came home? Yet even thinking like that, even for a split second, didn't feel right either. My thoughts were flitting with no logic, only chaos. I'd try to distract myself with a bit of TV, but I couldn't focus on it for long enough for it to make any sense. I'm a real water baby and like nothing more than a long soak in the bath – really long – but even that didn't take anything away. As soon as I got into the bath, the thoughts would come and I'd get out again.

As a child, I'd mastered hiding my emotions from as early as I can remember, but in the pit of loneliness that I was in, they wanted to come out, be released from their mental cage. My heart and body felt like it was going to explode, my chest so tight I'd be gasping for breath and my clothes soaked through with sweat. I'd be hot one minute and shivering the next and my bloody guts were a right mess. For me it was easier to disassociate from my reality altogether as often as I could. It was wrong and unhealthy, but it was my short-term, solving, coping mechanism.

No one knew the real extent of how I was when no one was around. I couldn't tell Michelle that from one journey to the next, from getting into the car to getting out of it again, I had no real memory of driving. She'd be shitting herself that I'd have a crash or something. The chances, in fairness, were high. I'd walk into where

147

Michelle was and try and smile at her, be with her, be what I thought she wanted, pushing the fears and worries back down as close to the pit of my stomach as I could get them, knowing full well that they'd be there to greet me again when I got home later.

38

With the news that there was an ICU neonatal cot at Birmingham City Hospital and that Michelle would be home, we could at last try getting back even a small percentage of normality, whatever that was. At least we'd be together. We'd spent over three weeks apart now, in a permanent state of deep and persistent grief and worry. Hearing the news that they were both going to be nearer had given me a glimmer of a new hope.

'Oh God, Michelle, that's just brilliant news. Just brilliant. I'm on my way to you. I'll be there in half an hour. When's it all gonna happen?'

'Not sure yet, they're just starting to make arrangements.'

I couldn't wait. I wanted to get there as fast as I could. I wanted to see her eyes and for her to see mine – the spark of lost joy that was going to flicker for those few seconds. I wanted to turn back and make the house perfect for Michelle coming home. I wanted to do everything! Michelle wouldn't give a shit about the house, but I wanted it to be nice for her.

She'd been living in a hospital room for nearly a month, so her homecoming was important. Her dream was to be coming home with twin girls. She'd be coming home empty handed for now, and I knew how much that was gonna sting. Even having Dana down the road would be a pull; she'd practically spent 24/7 at her incubator and now she was expected to be miles and minutes away from her instead of seconds.

Within what felt like only ten minutes, my phone rang again. Michelle's name appeared. Great, I thought, more details. It must be happening soon.

'The cot's gone. It's gone!' she said, her voice trying desperately to hide the obvious disappointment. 'They've had to give it to another baby. We're not coming home!'

'What do you mean? Are they allowed to do that? How come?' The glimmer of joy disappeared and a flood of disappointment swelled in.

'It just happens like that sometimes,' she said. 'They have to give it to a sick baby who's in that hospital because Dana's doing okay here. There's no urgency to move her.'

'Fuck!'

'I know. It's so disappointing. I'm so sorry to have to even say it. I know you'll be driving along all excited.'

'I know. I thought you were gonna be coming home with me. Shit!'

'It'll be our turn soon, hon. It's just not now.'

I drove the rest of the journey with my face low. That'd teach me to get my hopes up! Fucking typical result for me that! The disappointment was spread all over Michelle's face when I arrived back at the hospital in Shrewsbury, but we both resigned ourselves to the reality that it was just how things worked, and we'd have to wait.

Sitting with Dana that afternoon, Michelle commented that her legs weren't as lively when she'd changed her nappy. Michelle seemed to notice everything, but there weren't any concerns from anyone else caring for her.

I'd been there about an hour when a nurse paced through. 'There's another cot. In Walsall Manor Hospital. They've got a cot for Dana!'

'Really? Have they really got one this time?'

'Yes, they really have. You're going home!'

Fucking hell! My emotions were completely shot. This was the best news. They were definitely coming home this time. 'Michelle, you'll need to go and pack. You'll be taking everything with you this time.'

I couldn't believe it, it was truly happening. Weirdly, within the happiness of the news came a quiet panic. Shit, this was gonna be all new again. Another hospital, new doctors and nurses. We'd now got to know the medics here in Shrewsbury, and they'd got to know us a bit, too, but change was about to happen again and we were off to the unknown and the unexpected.

Things moved pretty quickly. The transporter incubator arrived in the intensive care room ready to be set up from Dana, and I instantly spotted a change in Michelle's face.

'That's what they took Alana away in,' was all she said.

We just stood and stared at it. I knew what was going through her mind. They'd put Alana in that in this very room and she'd never survived.

'Dana's coming nearer home though,' I told her, trying to be as reassuring as was possible. 'It's not the same. This is good news.'

I wasn't sure how much I believed what I was saying, though. Dana was still very tiny and very fragile. I had no idea what the journey back home would bring for her. Having Michelle next to me made my panic less obvious but I knew that it was only caged in.

'I know. It's just not nice seeing it again.'

'I bet.'

All we could do was give each other a hug.

Michelle's stuff didn't take long to pack up into carrier bags, and I started to fill the car. It was really going to happen now.

The nurses were carefully preparing Dana for her testing journey ahead. As they lifted her from her incubator, the only home she'd known, into the transporter incubator, my heart almost stopped beating.

She was so, so tiny, wide-eyed, fragile and scared looking. I didn't like it. It made my stomach sick with concern. Her large, black pupils stared out at us. It must have been so disturbing and upsetting for her, but she made no sound, no cry and showed no sign of discomfort. Before I knew it, her tubes and wired had all been reattached and she was getting settled in her temporary home. They'd need to make sure all of her levels had readjusted and then she'd be ready to go very shortly.

We'd decided that Michelle would go in the ambulance with her and I was going to meet her back in Walsall, only half a dozen miles from home. I wasn't certain where it was, but I knew the surrounding area and knew that the sign posts would direct me when I got nearer.

I could feel the anticipation of leaving, of saying goodbye and thank you, the unequivocal gratefulness that couldn't be expressed in a two-minute goodbye, but time was not on my side. I'd have to say the quick thank-yous now as we were getting ready to leave. Thankfully the entire focus was on Dana, and rightly so. My gratitude would come and be quickly gone.

As we sat awaiting the arrival of the ambulance, one of the doctors came to talk to us. I assumed that she was coming to say goodbye or pass on some information about Dana. Instead, she was about to deliver another stunningly painful blow to the two of us.

'I'm so sorry, but Dana's blood tests results have come back from this morning and, we've decided that it's not safe for her to travel at the moment.'

'What? What's happened?' we both asked.

'I'm afraid some of her levels are looking a little unstable and her platelet count is down. It's much safer if we keep her here and monitor her here before she goes.'

Fuck! Fuck again!

Was this really happening? Was this really being turned on its head? Again? This was emotional cruelty! What the fuck was I meant to do now? Even the staff in the neonatal ward couldn't believe it, either, but it was ok. It had to be. Dana needed to stay a bit longer to be assessed so that was what we'd be doing.

'So what happens to the cot in Walsall Manor? Will that go, too?'

'We've no way of knowing that,' said the doctor, 'but we'll see what happens next with Dana and we'll let them know that she'll hopefully be coming at some point. It just won't be today I'm afraid.'

So that was it.

No sooner had they settled Dana into the transporter incubator than they were back setting up her original 'home' with tubes and wires. Within minutes, she was back, settled once again. In a strange way, it was a relief to see her being put back in. I know, that's a weird thing to write, considering I was so desperate to get her closer to home, but it was definitely relief – pure relief. She was safe again. She looked familiar in there, it was where she 'belonged'. It looked right, the same. She wouldn't have to endure the long journey in the ambulance in Alana's incubator, and nor would me and Michelle have the upheaval of some place new and unfamiliar, another hospital and staff. Dana was obviously meant to be here for a bit longer.

'I guess I'll have to unpack the car again then!' I said, half laughing. 'Good job I hadn't done it all, eh!'

We were back to sitting with Dana. One of the doctors came in to speak to us. My adrenalin started pumping around my body once again.

'Because her platelets are down, we'll need to give her a transfusion,' she said. 'That can be dangerous in little ones, but we need to do it for her. We're also a bit concerned about the chance of infection developing in her gut, so we'll put her on antibiotics, too. We'll keep her a close eye on her.'

Should I have been worried? More worried than I already was? Had been? The doctors seemed to have it under control. 'When will the transfusion start? Soon?'

'Within the next couple of hours. It'll be coming from Birmingham, so we'll have to wait for the delivery.' The irony. Dana's blood coming from Birmingham, the place where we were all meant to be heading. 'It'll take a few hours for it to transfuse, too. It has to be done slowly. We'll know more then.'

The blood duly arrived in the late afternoon and was transfused over the hours that followed. Because of the threat of infection – the same type that we'd been warned about right back at the very beginning when the Bears were born – Dana's oxygen levels were decreasing and her oxygen intake had to be increased. That made me worry more but I was still full of hope, and the prospect of going home still hung in the air.

39

They tried to send me and Michelle away for something to eat, but it was fruitless. We walked as far as the cafeteria, ordered tea and toast, and sat for a minute staring at it before agreeing that we needed to go back. Being away from Dana was just too hard.

I remember walking back into the intensive care room and glancing at some of the carrier bags I'd brought back in, now dumped in the corner. How circumstances had so rapidly changed.

There were people coming and going and checking Dana constantly. We sat with her, staring, praying for an improvement and a successful transfusion. We made phone calls to correct the earlier ones we'd made, telling friends and family we weren't coming home after all. Just saying it out loud was hard. Everyone around us wanted there to be some joy, something positive to focus on, but it had turned, and now Dana had become unwell within hours. No one said too much, or if they did I started to not hear.

I was sinking slowly back to the place I was with Alana. Don't tell me anything unless it's good, I don't want to hear. Just tell me that she's getting well, that the transfusion worked and that the infection is under control. She'd been on antibiotics before and they'd worked, so there was no reason for these ones not to work. She lay so still, the energy drained from her. There was no moving of her hands or the flick of her foot or leg. She lay still.

I couldn't help myself: *Come on, God, do your job and help her out!*

As evening drew into the night, we remained sitting with her as she lay in the incubator.

'Is she crying, Michelle? Is she whimpering? Can you hear her?'

I hadn't heard her cry before. She'd never cried while I was there in the last three and a half weeks.

'A little.'

'Is she in pain? Does it mean she's in pain? You need to tell them. They need to do something for her!' I felt sheer panic and helplessness.

'Sometimes she does cry a bit,' Michelle tried to pacify me.

The whimpering was short-lived and I was glad, but my concern for Dana wasn't. As the night progressed, there was more to come.

'Dana's oxygen levels are not being sustained through her CPap tubes,' said another doctor. 'We're going to ventilate her to help keep the levels up.'

'We know what you're going to do,' I said. 'They did the same to Alana in the Children's Hospital. You're going to vibrate her little body, aren't you?'

'Yes, that's the one.'

Oh my God! Please God, don't be sending us down the same path!

This was déjà vu. It hadn't worked for Alana, but it had to work for Dana. I knew it was not good, not good at all. I had no words. What words would make a difference? It had only been just over three weeks since another doctor, in another hospital, had said similar words to try and save Alana.

'We're also worried about her tummy area, as it's become very swollen,' the doctor continued. 'That's where we think the infection is, but we'll have to watch the pressure of the swelling on her body.'

Oh shit, they were right. As you looked at her tiny body, her belly was proportionally huge in comparison.

'So what can you do about that?' I asked.

'We're giving her medicines to help, but if they aren't looking like they're successful we may have to call for the on-call consultant to come in from home again, and see what she thinks.'

That's what they did. Dr Wendy Tyler arrived at about 2am and it was then we knew that Dana's condition was seriously deteriorating. Her little body was vibrating gently at a rapid pace, but her once bright eyes were dim and lifeless. She was really fighting for her life and we knew it. Before she left, Dr Tyler spoke to us both.

'Try and get some rest, both of you. Dana's got a long journey ahead to fight and she'll need you to be beside her. Just try and rest for a while, even if it is for just an hour or two.'

Logically, I knew exactly what she was talking about. We were totally drained and exhausted, but fear of missing a moment now meant that sleep was the furthest thing from our minds and hadn't occurred to either of us.

'Why don't you sleep for an hour and then I'll sleep for an hour?' suggested Michelle. 'We'll make sure that one of us is here all of the time while the other one has a lie down?' I knew she wouldn't be the first volunteer to go, so, reluctantly, I went. Lying on Michelle's bed in her hospital room, the force of the exhaustion knocked me out. I was asleep within seconds.

The next thing I knew, Michelle was waking me up. It was about an hour-and-a-half since I'd seen Dana, but there was no change – not for the better anyway. They were still very concerned about her and were monitoring her very closely. Now it was Michelle's turn. I knew that she really didn't want to leave Dana.

'Please make sure it's just for an hour,' she demanded. 'Please don't let it go past an hour.'

'I promise, I'll wake you up, honestly.' It was my turn to reassure her now.

It was just me and Dana now. Time for the two of us to be together – amid the hustle and bustle of the medical team, evidently, but still me and her. My time. Her time. I sat and stared and prayed to whatever God existed that he would spare Dana and make her well again. She'd fought so hard already; I just wanted her to have another fight inside her.

Come on, Dana, you can do it, I said to myself.

I even spoke to Alana: 'Come and be with your sister, Alana! She needs you! Be with her and help her to get well.' I wanted her to listen and hear me from wherever she was.

Time was passing at different paces at different stages. Sometimes I'd catch the clock and wonder where the minutes had gone, and sometimes the hands of the clock didn't seem to have moved at all.

I realised that the number of beeps coming from Dana's monitor were more frequent, more urgent and suddenly there were more people gathering around her incubator.

'What's happening?' I asked.

I instinctively backed away from where I was sitting to give the medics more room, but was lost in the array of hand movements and fraught conversations that were going on. Through the glaze of the incubator and between the movements of arms and wires, I could see that they were beginning to manually resuscitate Dana.

She's gonna die! She's gonna die! was all I could think. *She's gonna die right now*, I was screaming inside.

I hadn't a clue what to do, and retreated to the corner of the room, almost paralysed in every sense. Where was Michelle? She needed to be here. Dana was going to die and Michelle wasn't here. How could I leave Dana to go and get her?

Her hour was up, but I couldn't leave. What if Dana died and neither of us was here with her? Panic seized every part of me. The medics continued to pump oxygen into Dana's lungs, willing her to live. A movement to my right made me glance away for a split second. Michelle was at the door. She saw the absolute panic in my eyes and her instant panic joined mine.

'Mum and Dad are both here,' announced a nurse. They obviously knew that Dana might not make it and wanted us both there for her.

'What's happening, Gary?'

'They've had to resuscitate Dana.'

I grabbed Michelle and for what felt like a lifetime, but was only a few seconds, we held each other. All we could do was sit and cry and hope. We knew what was coming. Surely there was no way back now – they'd been resuscitating her for over ten minutes – but I was wrong.

'We've got her back. We've got her back,' shouted another nurse.

Oh my God, I couldn't believe it. Had she really made it? Was she really gonna make it? Myself and Michelle just looked at each other through our tears and allowed the professionals to keep working around Dana. She was alive. *Come on, Dana, you can do it!*

Her little body continued to vibrate as it was ventilated. The doctor came to speak to us again about how grave the situation was. The words weren't what I wanted to hear and didn't register. As far as I was concerned, she was breathing and that was hope.

'We just ask one thing.' Michelle said. 'If she's about to die, can you make sure that we're here? We don't want her to die on her own.'

'Of course,' was all that was said.

By now, the low sun was creeping in the window, and there was a changeover of staff, thankfully all familiar to us.

Everyone was worried for us and yet, they also gave us a glimmer of hope in that tiny babies bounced back much quicker than adults, which was fact. I was more than happy to hold on to that.

40

Dana's belly was still really swollen, and whatever they were trying to do via the drugs just wasn't working. The doctors wanted to do surgery on her gut, but that just wasn't possible in Shrewsbury. The Children's Hospital back in Birmingham was mentioned, too, but Dana just wasn't stable enough to travel. Alana had been really, really sick and she'd been fit to travel – just. Dana must have been even worse then as they weren't gonna risk moving her until there were signs of improvement.

We continued to sit and stare and pray. Surely God wouldn't take both our children? Was he really that cruel? Did I deserve this? Was it karma for past wrongs? Michelle certainly didn't. Dana's deterioration had come on so quickly. One minute she was in the transporter incubator and a dozen or more hours later she was being resuscitated. The whole thing was so hard to even begin to get my head around. Could her recovery be just as quick? In another dozen hours would we be looking back at this horrific time?

Wendy Tyler was now back on duty, after just a few hours away, and came to see us. We were so grateful for her time. I know it's their job to do what they do, but who wants to be called out of bed at 2am, then return home for a couple of hours sleep, and still able to be polite and professional throughout? She must have been shattered, too.

'There is one thing we can try.'

Déjà vu again. I'd heard that one before as well.

'If I'm able to get a drain into Dana's gut, that would relieve the pressure inside and maybe enable her to recover enough for us to get her transferred for the surgery that she needs.'

'Thank you so much,' we both replied. 'Of course you need to try.'

'It does come with dangers, though. It might be that when I make the opening, the gut could already be too damaged for me to do anything.'

This wasn't looking like the way out that Dana needed, bless her, but I wanted her to have every chance of recovering, every chance of making it back to us.

'We understand. Please just come and get us if she'd not gonna make it. Please don't let her die on her own.' Again, we were reassured that this would be the case.

The hardest part for me was yet to come. Saying goodbye to Dana, knowing that this might be the last time I'd see her alive, but hoping and praying that it wasn't going to be was heart-breaking. She looked so gravely ill. Her skin had lost its colour and her beautiful dark eyes were vacant.

'Love you so much, Dana. Come on, you can do it. Keep fighting,' I whispered in to her ear.

We took the slow walk back to Michelle's empty room. Half of her things were in the car and half in the intensive care room with Dana. It was like we'd never been in here before. What the fuck were we meant to do now? Just sit and wait? Talk? Stay silent? I remember lying down on the bed and looking across at Michelle standing against the wall.

'Come and sit down, Michelle. There's nothing we can do now but wait and hope that she's gonna come out of it.'

'I can't. I need to be ready in case they come back in.'

Every noise coming from the wards around make Michelle physically jump. I closed my eyes to try and keep the bile from my stomach coming up into my mouth. Panic, exhaustion, lack of food, distress and the prospect of losing Dana were overwhelming.

Within twenty or so minutes, the door to the room opened. I wanted to see a confident face, a face of someone with encouraging news. Instead, it was the opposite.

'You need to come,' said the nurse. 'Dana hasn't responded very well.'

No! Not again! No!

There were no further words from any of us. None of us could speak. Me and Michelle just cried and walked. How my legs carried me back there I will never know. I may as well have been walking to the gallows. I knew that what was going to greet me was the death of my second daughter, my little Dana, my Little Bear.

The nurse, Carol, led us out to where Dana was. There were still lots of people around her. Dr Tyler turned as we came in.

'I'm so, so sorry. When I opened her up, her gut was already dead.'

'Please stop now,' Michelle sobbed. 'Please let us have her. Please let her be with her mom and dad now.'

Heartbreak.

I was distraught. My whole body was slumped with lack of a reason to live. People were rallying around us, trying to get chairs for us to sit in while we held Dana in her final minutes. She was wrapped in blankets and shawls and, leaving her incubator, the only home that she'd ever known, she was handed to Michelle.

Nativity scene number two. It was hard to believe that this was really happening. My daughter was going to die. Right here, right now. I was going to lose her. Everything that I had planned to do with Dana and all the milestones that I'd wanted to be alive to see were now being crushed with every last breath that she took. As with Alana, they continued to manually ventilate her as she slipped away.

'I love you Dana, go and be with Alana.' Michelle repeated over and over and over again.

'I love you, Dana. I love you, Little Bear,' I repeated, too, but the lump in my throat was so huge that the sound was strained and full of emotion.

My Little Bear, Dana, died at 12.30pm on Tuesday 11th November. She was 26 days old.

Sisters together again, in heaven.

41

We sat with Dana and cuddled her. Unlike with Alana, I felt able and wanted to hold Dana in my arms, not just hold her with Michelle's arms around her, too.

She was just so light and fragile. It was hard to believe she was any weight at all. I held her, kissed her and told her how much I loved her. Inside, my thoughts were crushing. My organs were crushing me. How was this really happening to me? To us?

God was that cruel after all. He'd taken Alana and now he'd taken Dana. How could he do this? This definitely wasn't the way it should have been. Dana should have been in Walsall Manor Hospital now, and Michelle and I should have been at home buying groceries and baby supplies, ready for when Dana was well enough to come home. Instead, we were here, with Dana in our arms, but she was gone. Both my Little Bears were gone now.

Another doctor came to us as we sat and she checked Dana's heart. There was no beat. We already knew.

'What we'd like to do is remove all of the tubes and lines now so that you can just be with her. We're going to ask you to leave while this takes place, if that's okay.'

I understood, but didn't want to go. I didn't want to leave her. I wanted them to leave her alone and leave her with me, but we were led back out and into the empty room again.

'It won't take long. She'll just needs a few stitches where the incision was made and you can go back to her.'

We thanked the nurse again and sat and broke our hearts together, sitting on the bed.

We didn't talk, we just cried and cried, loud sobbing cries. Tears for Dana, tears for Alana, tears for a life that could never be the same again. I wanted God to take me, too, there and then. I wanted to be with my Little Bears above anything else.

'We're gonna have to ring people again, aren't we?' I said.

There was no one around this time. We were far from home, and Dana's deterioration had been so swift it had been hard to update people without compromising time with Dana. Now we had no choice. I phoned Michael; Michelle phoned her parents, then other members of her family, and finally, her best friend. Everyone was in deep shock and distress for us. No one could believe that both our girls had been taken away from us, especially Dana, who had been doing so well – and she had been. Playing with her in the sun became a distant memory now. Daddy and Dana playing in the sun. Never to happen again.

We were able to go back in to Dana pretty swiftly. They'd wrapped her up, changed her nappy, replacing her tiny one with one fit for a normal, healthy-sized baby to cover the stitches. It made her look even tinier lying within it. She looked peaceful. Free of pain and tubes and being prodded. She just looked like a beautiful, tiny, sleeping baby, content and without a care in the world.

We washed and changed her, and just keep loving her for as long as the moments lasted. The hospital gave us a babygrow as we hadn't anything with us – she'd only worn small vests in her incubator as it was easier for the staff to get to her and monitor her without too many clothes on, and the matching babygrow to the one we'd dressed Alana in – the yellow 'Good things come in small packages' one – was back in Birmingham. They found a pretty pink and white gingham one. It was showing signs of wear from the other baby girls who had needed to borrow it in the past, but it was all we had and it was just perfect. It was cosy and would keep her warm.

'Would you like us to take prints of her hands and feet for you, and a lock of her hair?'

'Yes, please.'

My heart was sinking to new lows as I answered. Another set of handprints, another set of footprints, another lock of hair in a tiny polythene bag. Another set of hands that I wouldn't hold, feet that wouldn't run to me, hair that would never be brushed.

Another set of photographs were taken. It still felt wrong to be photographing a dead child, but they would be the only memories we'd have now. We had Alana's and now we had Dana's, but there'd be no school, graduation or wedding photos. These were the only photos we'd ever have and that made them so, so precious.

As much as I felt uncomfortable with having a photo taken with Dana, I also needed it more than anything. I was sure that one day I'd be able to look back on the photos and know how precious my time with her had been, that she'd really been in this world, really been a part of my life, and that I'd really been her dad.

By now, some of Michelle's family had arrived – so loyal, the epitome of commitment to the notion of family and love – and her best friend had come, too. One by one, they arrived to say goodbye to Dana: their granddaughter, their niece, the child of their best friend. Everyone was distraught and shell-shocked.

Dana's death had crept up on everyone without warning, and there was a huge feeling of disbelief in the air. Even the staff who had looked after Dana were devastated for us, knowing that we'd arrived as a family of four nearly a month ago, and would now be leaving as a lonely, broken family of two.

The intensive care room was quiet now. No beeps or hustle and bustle. That was where we had to leave Dana now, in the room she'd spent her whole life in.

There was no walking her down to the mortuary; that wasn't allowed here. Eventually, we had to love and hold her for the last time and walk away, unable to think clearly enough to really thank the staff for everything that they had done for the Bears and for Michelle.

When we walked out of the room and along the corridor, it felt like lightening really did strike twice. It was completely surreal. How could I just leave Dana there for someone else to take her to the mortuary? She'd be with someone who didn't know her or care about her like I did. But I kept walking, and went along with the wrongness of it all.

I glanced at the other neonatal side rooms as I went, the rooms that I'd hoped Alana and Dana would have occupied before their return home. I knew the drill – the nearer to the 'way out' of the neonatal ward you were, the nearer you were to getting home. We were near the door now, but without the luggage that we'd so wanted to carry in baby car seats and blankets. Instead, I carried the remnants of Michelle's things that were still to be put in the boot of the car, a worthless bundle. I felt lost. Lost within myself, not knowing what to do or think.

As we headed for the exit, I looked around the familiarity of the entrance area to the maternity department: the seating area, the tiny kiosk where you could buy a cuppa, the shop selling baby clothes and cards – the same shop I'd bought teddies for my Little Bears and a 'twins' card for Michelle. It was so familiar, where people had come to visit me and Michelle, where I'd spent time chatting with Michelle over coffee, a break from staring at the incubators, somewhere close by, but a rest away from the norm. As I looked around, I knew I'd never want to come back here again. I didn't want to see any of this again.

Michelle's family and her best friend were waiting for us when we came out. Everyone felt awkward in their heartbreak and no one knew what to say or whether we were gonna sit down or go straight home. No words from anyone would have been adequate anyway, it was just so awfully wrong. It was finished now. There was no going back in time, no repeat button, no trying to get my family back.

Strangers mulled around the entrance, none of them knowing the excruciating grief that we were exposed to. Now, I was going to have to find the courage and focus to drive the sixty miles home. I'm sure someone probably offered to drive the car from me, I can't recall, but I would have refused anyway.

I just wanted to be at home now, away from everyone's glaring eyes, where I could bury my head in the proverbial sand and never look up to the sky again, never speak to anyone again and never come up for air. My body was crushing me with emotion. Even the normal, everyday task of going to the parking ticket machine to get a ticket validated was taxing and confusing to me, pointless. I knew that this was going to be my last journey home from here. I wouldn't be coming back tomorrow, like I'd been doing for nearly a month, I hoped I'd never come back. It would be just too hard.

42

We both cried as we drove home, the shock and sorrow of the whole situation enveloping us further. We didn't talk, not really. I didn't have a clue what I was going to do next, or what I was meant to do.

Just keep driving... just keep driving... concentrate... just keep driving.

I didn't want this situation to become more of a catastrophe by adding a car crash to it, but dark thoughts within me were saying had Michelle not have been in the car with me, then there would've been every chance I wouldn't have made it home. I'd have happily driven my car off the road and gone into oblivion to be with the Bears.

When I opened the front door to our home it was even worse. The house was cold, because it was late November, and because none of us had lived there properly for the best part of a month. Cold because there was a lack of love anywhere around the place.

Michelle just shuffled from room to room, familiarising herself once again with a home she'd last seen properly nearly a month ago. There was no noise, and no sound. The silence was deafening.

What the fuck were we meant to do now? Scream? Cry? Watch TV?

Nothing felt right. Nothing *was* right.

'What are we meant to do now, Bear?' I asked Michelle.

Nothing came but more tears. Neither of us knew what to do. We just sat for a moment on the settees and stared into space.

'Shall we go to Mom's? Be around people for a bit?' she eventually whispered.

I agreed we'd go round to see her mum and dad, not having the foggiest idea if I really did agree with doing so or just had no better alternative to offer in response. Michelle's parents only lived round the corner, so we walked.

We held hands, but still couldn't bear to say many words to each other. It was just too hard. Her mum's house was always welcoming and, like true families do, other family members had come together to share their grief and shock. I remember clearly the haunting sound of Michelle's screaming cries to her sister, Carol, coming from the living room while the rest of us sat in near silence in the kitchen.

'What am I gonna do!' she cried out. 'What am I gonna do! I've got no babies! I've got no babies!'

Silence fell in the whole house and heads lowered in grief and heartbreak.

'I've got all this milk to give them and no babies! I've got no babies!' Her grief stripped the lining of her throat as she broke down further.

The cries and wailing from her were excruciating to listen to. It made my heart feel like it was about to explode, the pressure of the pain inside bursting through. How were we ever going to get through this? How was anything ever going to be important again? I wish I had an answer for her. What was she gonna do? She was right. She had no babies. I had no babies. No one had any answers, just excruciating grief.

Eventually, the two of them – Michelle and her sister – joined us in the kitchen, walking in to the silence broken only by the whispering sound of the rest of us sniffling in our grief. Someone made tea. Someone always makes tea. We didn't really drink it, nor did we really talk. I wanted to leave. Coming here was the right thing to do, but now I needed to escape again now, or so I thought. I hadn't a clue really.

Michelle broke the silence: 'We're going to have to go back to Shrewsbury to register Dana's death as well, Gary. That'll have to be done at some point.'

I knew that meant me. I knew this was my job. I knew that this was what I'd done for Alana and I would do again for Dana, but going back there was the last thing I wanted to do. I didn't want to go anywhere near that M6-M54 motorway route again, the same junctions, the same signs telling me how many miles I had to go, the same traffic hotspots and roundabouts.

Did it really need to be done soon? Couldn't it wait? Could someone else do it? No, no they couldn't. I was her daddy and it was going to be my job. I'd done it for Alana and now I would have to pull myself together enough to do it for Dana, too.

'I'll do it tomorrow,' I said, after a long pause.

We left, still hoping our steps would lead us somewhere else but knowing that we needed to go home. Thankfully, darkness was falling even though it was still relatively early. It gave us cover, as we walked the short distance home. There was nothing else for us to do. No roles, no purpose.

We sat on the settee and hugged for a while. Michelle said that we'd probably need to eat something, but I had absolutely no appetite at all and I'm not sure she did either. We decided to go to bed. It was still early but at least in bed the prospect of today coming to an end was nearer. We could lock out the world and encourage this awful day to end. I went up first. I could hear Michelle crying alone downstairs, but as much as I wanted to go down to her, as much as I needed her to know that I cared how she felt and that we were in this together, I couldn't go down. I just couldn't.

Her grief and mine, mixed together, was like a bomb waiting to explode and I just couldn't go down to her. I had an overwhelming sense of blame. It was all my fault. All of it. If Michelle hadn't have met me then none of this would've happened. The Bears wouldn't be dead and Michelle wouldn't be downstairs, alone, grieving for her two beautiful baby girls.

Even when she arrived upstairs a bit later, we didn't speak, me pretending to be half asleep.

Michelle got into bed, turned off the light, and took off her glasses.

We lay there together but very much apart in what we were going through. I just wanted to shut my eyes and hope this nightmare that had landed at my door was just that: a nightmare. In all honesty, I hoped that when I shut my eyes that they wouldn't open in the morning, and I wouldn't wake up at all.

Tomorrow would be another day with or without me in it. It would still be the first new day without either of the Bears. The first day of the rest of our lives.

But I did wake up the following morning, the nightmare was real. Michelle was crying in bed before we'd even got up. I needed to get up and try to find some purpose for the day, no matter how little or insignificant that purpose was.

Then Michael arrived. He'd driven down from home again to be with us and lend his support. Amazing. Much as I loved Michelle's family, having Michael down was exactly what I needed, someone who knew me inside and out, someone who placed no expectations

167

on me, someone who could make me laugh with banter even on a day like today. He was family to me and it was great to have him around. Michelle had her family and friends around her, always wanting to do whatever it took, and now I had mine, Michael.

It was with a heavy heart that the journey I vowed never to drive again was the one I was now gonna be taking for 'tomorrow' was here. Having Michael with me for company again made it less traumatic and more functional, though. We didn't talk that much as we drove, but he cracked the usual jokes, and told some funny tales from home. Against all expectation, I found myself smiling and laughing. Weird really, when the last thing you think you want to do is laugh, but the body and the brain just seem to do it so naturally.

Eventually we found the place where we were meant to be. I had in my hand Dana's birth certificate on cream paper and her death certificate on green paper. Reality really hit then. My emotions were packed so tightly under the surface I was worried they might burst out.

At least this time, there was no queue. In Birmingham, there had been so many people around, which was the last thing I needed. Although nothing had changed, this time I was more aware. I knew what was going to happen and I knew what to do.

That in itself was so sad. Just muttering the words that your baby daughters had both now died was so heart-breaking. Surreal words, like they were coming out of someone else's mouth. The lady that we saw was so professional, offering compassion and empathy that was so needed. There was a genuine expression of sadness on her face and sincerity in her words. How those people do that job every day I just don't know.

Thoughts of my own family came and went. Mostly went. There was no way that I was gonna ring my mum and tell her that Dana had also died. No way. I felt no guilt for feeling that way. She'd shown her cards yet again after Alana's death.

Would she change the cards she held, and reach out to me if I gave her one more chance? As much as the little boy inside me was tempted, I wasn't prepared to risk it. Not this soon again. Instead, Michelle's mum said that she'd ring her and tell her for me – one grandmother to another. I'm sure there were a few specially chosen words said from this end, and Mum did say that she'd be in touch about the funeral. She never did.

Since the episode with Dad, Michelle had spoken to him and had a very emotional, heart-to-heart with him – again, from the payphone in the corridor outside the neonatal ward, pound coins clunking in as they spoke. I'd wanted her to speak to him. I felt bad about what had happened to him. My typical go-to mental pattern told me that I needed to blame myself for his collapse, yet my thoughts continued to contradict each other. He deserved it/he didn't deserve it, I deserved it/I didn't deserve it. I'd beat myself up for being horrible to him and then beat myself for being nice about him. I couldn't win. After everything, he'd had the balls to say to Michelle on the phone that he wanted to be part of our lives: mine, Michelle's and Dana's.

I'd believe it when it happened, but now Dana had died there'd be just me and Michelle again. Anyway, I felt he had a right to know about Dana. Michelle's mum rang him, too.

43

The return to Shrewsbury experience now over and it was time to organise another funeral, a second within weeks of the first. Organising a funeral for one child is hard enough, but having to do it for a second, and within a month, was as hard an emotional experience as you could imagine.

It was another, extreme déjà vu moment in my life, and me and Michelle attended the appointment with the funeral directors together this time. They were genuinely upset for us that we were back so soon for another child, their sympathy clear in their stares; but however traumatic and unfair the situation, Dana's funeral had to be arranged.

As much as we didn't want to go through another funeral, and would have happily buried our heads, we also knew that what we'd done for Alana we would certainly do for Dana. She would have the same funeral arrangements as her sister.

It was all so surreal yet again. Every question asked by the undertakers was answered with, 'Yes, we'll have that again... yes, we'll have the same coffin... yes, we'll have the same crucifix design... plaque... cars... readings... flowers...' It went on and on, in the same vein. However, there was a real sticking point that took my breath away: the undertakers weren't sure if we'd be able to bury Dana alongside Alana, in the same grave.

'What? We can't bury them together?' I asked, trying to hide my frustration and panic. 'They can't be buried separately! What do you mean? They need to be together. Surely they can put another little coffin in with Alana?'

It was clear to see how distressing this was going to be for us both. Looking back, it must have been as hard for the undertakers to explain as it was for us to comprehend, but Alana's grave was not a 'double' grave, so the undertakers, rightly, had to warn us that there might be red tape and regulations that would mean that Dana would have to be buried in a different grave. They were unsure if the council would let them reopen Alana's grave to bury Dana with her.

This was devastating. Surely they wouldn't be cruel enough to say that the twins had to be buried apart? The vision of Alana's grave plot flashed up in my head. The plots either side had already been taken, so we couldn't even buy the grave plot right next to her if the answer was a no.

We just wanted them to be buried together, to be back together. They needed to be together again and we needed them to be together again. It didn't bear thinking about having to eventually visit two graves either. They said they'd do their best and get back to us later that day with the decision. I prayed and prayed that the answer from them would allow my girls to be side by side.

Later in the afternoon the phone rang: 'Mr. Anderson, the council have agreed to let you bury Dana with Alana in the same grave.'

I cannot start to tell you how relieved I felt. Because of Dana's small size, they were going to allow Alana's grave to be opened so that Dana could be buried with her sister. It was how it was meant to be. Together again. Together forever.

We were able to visit Dana in the chapel of rest, like we'd done with Alana. I still remember how cold she was. I knew she'd be cold, of course, but the reality of the coldness never leaves you. I wanted to kiss her and hold her and take her out of her coffin, to keep her warm, let her feel how much love I had for her, put my daddy arms around her and keep her safe.

I wanted to talk to her, scream out loud in grief, stare at her, anything, but she lay there, imitating sleep, motionless and colourless. We put her blanket in with her, her name clearly written in embroidery, with a picture of Alana and rosary beads. It was heart-breaking.

All the time I was bracing myself for her funeral. I dreaded it.

To say that it came and went in a blur is an understatement. It was just too much to take in. Super-turbo autopilot had well and truly kicked in. When I recall it now, I'm not quite certain whether I am recalling Alana's funeral or Dana's funeral. They were identical in service and structure, but separated by emotional heartache.

My friends returned, both from home and those that I'd made in Birmingham. Their support meant so much to me. Michelle's family and friends regathered again, too, to support us, many helping us to organise the funeral and music for the church again. It must have been déjà vu for everyone actually. Most faces showed disbelief and looks of sympathy that said: *I can't believe we're here again.*

The service took place with the respect that was needed and deserved, and before we knew it, we were back at Alana's graveside ready to bury Dana. I cannot even begin to express how awful it was to be there looking in to the grave of my dead daughter Alana knowing that she was just there under a bunch of soil and I was there to place her twin sister on top of her. The physical pain within was excruciating, crushing.

The pallbearers weren't overly keen on me placing Dana into the grave, but it wasn't very deep now and I reassured them that I would do it with the upmost care, so they let me do it. Letting go of her coffin was the hardest. The end. If I could have fallen into that grave with her, I would have. The grains of soil could fall on me; I'd have been happy to end my life there and then.

I knew that those around me would be looking on and despairing at the sight. I felt sorry for them in that moment as I glanced up – most of them sniffling and shivering in equal measure – there seemed to be so many. I remember thinking that they needed to be back in their cars so that they could warm up. As much as I wanted to stay, I also wanted desperately to leave not for them, but for me. I needed space to breath.

Neither me nor Michelle spoke in the car on the way back to the wake, which had been prepared and set out exactly like Alana's had been. There were no words. We just held hands.

People drank tea and sympathised with us. Mum didn't show of course. Dad neither. In fact, none of my family came.

My friends bent over backwards to take the time off and get here wherever possible, but my family hadn't. People often wonder why my friends are so important to me. Well, this was why. They were here for me, like they'd been all my life, through thick and thin, keeping me going – keeping me alive, in fact, on many occasions without even realising it.

My family weren't here. In fact, my Dad's excuse, later, was that he hadn't been 'invited'. Invited? I've been to dozens of funerals and never had an invite to one of them. Invited! What the fuck? Your granddaughter is being buried – now your second granddaughter is being buried – and you want an invite to her funeral? I know they would have justified it with saying that they weren't sure if they'd have been made welcome, but for fuck's sake, it was their grandchildren. Family ties could have been repaired maybe if they'd have come, but they decided they couldn't make it.

As an aside, I did have another granddad – Mum's dad – and a huge extended family of aunts and uncles and cousins in Hartlepool who I'd only met as an adult. They'd welcomed me with open arms, and I kept in touch with them periodically, but I didn't have the courage to phone any of them and let them know about what had been happening with the Bears. I was embarrassed about my poor mental health and didn't want them to know how unwell I was. I was so ashamed and embarrassed of who I was. In my head I believed no one would like me, never mind love me, if they found out

As much as I missed and wanted family around, I don't think I could have coped with the internal pressure of them being here. I would have been embarrassed and ashamed if they'd come and my own parents hadn't. It would just cement own mum and dad's absence. I know my Hartlepool family would have come, without a shadow of a doubt, if I'd have let them know. They'd been nothing other than accepting and caring toward me, but I just found it too hard and emotional to make contact. I felt unable to accept their support and love. Not right now, anyway.

With the wake drawing to a close, it was time for everyone to go home, to return to their normal lives with their families. My friends from home were leaving, too. They'd now be 300 miles away again. I was so sad to see them go and missed them already. I was back to feeling alone again – strange, when I was still surrounded by people who cared.

I felt completely lost. What was I meant to do now? I'd spent six months on a pregnancy treadmill that had suddenly stopped and I'd been thrown off the back, crumpled, injured and emotionally scarred for life. Two deaths, then two burials of the most precious gifts of life ever bestowed on me. How was I ever meant to 'get on with it'? How were me and Michelle meant to even remember what a normal life was, let alone live it?

44

One thing was for certain: there was plenty of thinking time now and, amidst all the grief and surrealism, my thoughts were also tugged back into thinking about when I might have to go back to work. While everything had been going on with Michelle and the Bears, I was actually awaiting a start date for a new job with the Royal Mail as part of its security team. I had also been one of the team that manned the doors at the Hyatt Hotel and Merchant Stores Bar in Birmingham at the weekend, which I'd had to put on hold, and now wondered when I'd feel able to return there, too.

Before the Bears were born, the Royal Mail had told me that I'd have to have training before I'd be able to start the job, and that I'd been booked in for that training on Monday, 20th October. On the morning that the Bears were born, I'd been looking forward to the training, but with what had happened subsequently I'd completely forgotten all about it, understandably.

They phoned me, obviously wondering why I hadn't turned up. They must have been a bit pissed off at having to chase me. I know I would have been if the shoe had been on the other foot. When I took the call, I tried to comprehend what the bloke on the other end of the phone was telling me, but every word just seemed like it took so long to process. All I was feeling was numbness, knowing that me even thinking about starting a new job wasn't going to happen.

'I'm so sorry! I'm so sorry! I totally forgot!' was all I could think of saying on the spot, my mind so shot with grief. This must have pissed them off a treat to hear that.

'What happened, Gary, why didn't you arrive this morning?'

'I'm so sorry! I can't come.' I paused not really knowing how to say the words. 'I'm really sorry, my baby daughter died yesterday. I forgot all about it. I'm so sorry!'

Then it was his turn to pause slightly. I mean, I'm sure he had prepared an answer to any of my possible excuses for not turning up, and had probably already formed an opinion of me as unreliable, unenthusiastic and half-hearted, someone who couldn't even be bothered to turn up for the first day of training. I'm sure he'd seen and hear plenty of excuses before today. However, having an answer to hand when you've just heard that the person you thought unreliable was in fact dealing with the most traumatic experience possible was, I'm sure, not run of the mill.

'Gary, I'm so sorry to hear that.' His voice was full of compassion. I bet he was thinking, *No wonder he didn't turn up.*

'I know. Thanks. She died last night.' I could hear the emotion in the undertones of my voice.

The conversation continued with more respectful interchanges. The bloke couldn't have been nicer, actually. To his credit, he took what I said as a professional would and said that he'd happily put me back on the training schedule that was happening in a month's time, that he still wanted me to come and work for them and asked if that seem reasonable to me.

It did. In my head, a month further down the line, Dana would be much better and growing well, and hopefully she'd be home with Michelle or as near as. I was dead grateful to the bloke. After all, he could have said that because I'd missed the training that I'd missed out, and that they'd have to offer the job to someone else. I thanked him and apologised again before the phone call ended.

Well now, another month had passed and another phone call came from the guy at the Royal Mail – more training days had been arranged and my name was on the list. What was I gonna say this time? It all sounded unreal – it was unreal.

'I'm so sorry again, my other daughter has died, as well. I'm not going to be able to do the training just yet. I'm so sorry.'

Every time I'd spoken to this bloke I'd had to tell him that another daughter had died, and that I was unable to attend. If it wasn't so real it would've made a good lie. The poor bloke on the other end of the phone must have thought, *Fuck me, that guy's having it bad*, or maybe less sympathetically, *Does he want this fucking job or what?*

'I completely understand if you have to give my job to someone else,' I said. 'I know that you can't just hold it open for me. Whatever you decide is okay, honestly.'

Dead daughters or not, they weren't going to hold the job open for me forever. I knew that at this point, no matter how hard I tried, there was no way that I would have been able to do training and concentrate enough to take anything in, or have the mental or physical energy to hold down a full-time job.

I'd always been a worker and for me to turn down a good job opportunity like this was not done easily or lightly. All credit to the bloke on the phone, he said he'd put me on the next training day available – it would be after Christmas now – but that they still wanted me to come and work for them. I did want to, accepting with gratitude and humbleness. People didn't have to be kind, but they were.

Meanwhile, my job on the doors at Merchant Stores and round the corner with Les at the Hyatt Hotel had been kept open for me, too. I usually did weekends and actually looked forward to going every week. The guys I did the doors with were good to be around and the staff around the bars I knew well too.

Just doing a Friday and a Saturday in familiar surroundings with familiar people was what I thought I needed, so the second weekend after Dana's funeral I was back on the doors. Sitting at home feeling sad and sorry for myself was not going to work for me. I needed to keep busy, I needed to be doing something.

The house was full of grief and pain. Any minute out of it was a slight relief, just to not have to feel the sorrowful atmosphere oozing through my skin. It wasn't anyone's fault, certainly not Michelle's, but I didn't want to be there. Anywhere else, in fact, would suffice, which is why I decided, after Dana's funeral, that I wanted to go back on the doors. I had a purpose again. Sure, I worried that people would judge me and say that it was too soon. Well actually, I suspected that lots of people did judge me silently. They were hardly gonna confront me with it, were they?

Michelle knew it was the right thing for me to do, so the decision was made, with her support. Normality, part one, resumed – but it wasn't easy. How could it be?

The easy bit was with the punters. They had no idea I was a grieving dad, so didn't give me that sympathetic look or compensate for me even in the smallest way. They just wanted to get into the pub or bar at the hotel with their friends and companions, drink and get inebriated at the bar, eat in the restaurant, lounge around or whatever.

It was the people that knew who were the hardest, though there weren't many of them in this setting. It was obvious to me who knew and who didn't. Those who did gave me that 'look': the silent look that wondered how I was doing, the look that wondered if I was gonna kick off, the look that wasn't sure if the conversation was too jovial, too sarcastic, too vulgar, too much for the vulnerable me. I know blokes are blokes and the 'look' probably didn't exist for more than a fleeting minute, but I was always expecting it.

My closest friend on the door was Les, of course. We'd known each other a while now and had hit it off straight away. We got each other's humour and had plenty in common; he was mad into self-defence and training like me. He was a family man, and he and his wife had been really supportive to me and Michelle throughout her pregnancy, and again after the twins had died.

He was the one who really knew what was going on with me. If I wanted to talk about everything that was going on at home, then he was happy to listen; but if I didn't, then we didn't, that was fine too. Talking about death, especially where babies were concerned, made people feel awkward so I was aware that I didn't want there to be any awkwardness around me. I knew Les was there for me if I needed him and always appreciated his honest, genuine friendship. I didn't want sympathy and Les was good at not giving it to me – exactly what I wanted.

Les got why I'd come back on the doors so soon after the Bears had died. I think if he'd been in my shoes he'd have come back as well. Going back on the doors felt like the right thing to do. It felt more manly than sitting at home doing fuck all. I couldn't bear the thought of people thinking that I was weak, making the Bears an excuse as to why I hadn't come back to work. Les also knew though that when push came to shove, no amount of grief would stop me from supporting him on the door, being competent in my job, resilient enough not to let him down when he needed me.

177

45

At home, things continued on autopilot. People came and went, family and friends wanted to give us space and leave us alone to have time together.

They were right. It was exactly what me and Michelle needed, but exactly what I didn't know what to do with. What was I going to talk about? We'd spent six months plus focusing on little else other than keeping the pregnancy going, then fighting on behalf of the Bears. Any conversation after that was almost meaningless and insignificant.

We watched some TV and tried to keep occupied with so much time on our hands. In one way, staying in was safe, away from the imaginary public glare. Staying in meant that I didn't feel like I was surrounded by placards and banners announcing that I was the grieving dad of not just of one child but two children, making the banners bigger and wider.

At the flip of a coin, however, staying home was stifling, really stifling, almost suffocating. If Michelle wanted to talk about the Bears, I could stomach it for a short time, and then the bile in my guts would rise and I'd want to leave the room, stop her from talking, silence her and shut her up. It sounds cruel and harsh, and I knew that it was, but my own sadness was already so consuming.

Sure, I knew that she was going through the same – her trauma was like my own – but I didn't want or need her to put it into words for me. Just looking at her spoke of a thousand sorrows, as it was written all over her face and demeanour. No words would ever reach the mark of how sad we both felt, but having her here, in front of me, talking about how she felt and her own all-consuming heartbreak was something I'd give anything to have washed aside and buried with the Bears.

It was clear that we were going to have very different ways of existing now. Michelle was living with her grief on her sleeve, expressing it freely and openly with those who cared for her; and then there was me, the complete opposite. The less expressive I could be, the better. The less open I could be, the better. The more I acted normal, the better. After all, I was the man of the house, the one expected to be strong and supportive to Michelle, and to take

178

everything on my shoulders. That was my expectation of myself, too, and I knew everyone else wanted me to be that way – or at least I thought I knew.

I had to watch my anger. It wasn't escaping all of the time, yet, but it wouldn't take much. It had already flown out a few times. It was like a monster, festering inside, deep within my veins. Someone cutting me up in their car, being rude to me, anything really, made the grief beast stir inside me. It'd already been unleashed once with guys around the corner, delivering grass, and I needed to make sure that it wasn't going to erupt with Michelle, or on the doors at work, or even in the supermarket or when I was putting petrol in the car.

I knew that there was no way that I could let it loose on Michelle. She didn't deserve that and it would have been so wrong. She'd already got caught in the crossfire with the grass guys. Anyway, she hadn't done anything wrong. She was just grieving like any mother would, but how was this gonna work now? She wanted to talk about the Bears, but I most certainly didn't want to. As far as I was concerned, the more I buried my head in the proverbial sand the better.

I wanted to get rid of my grief and pain and the way I thought the best way was to try and push it away, or hide it within, or try to ignore it and act like it wasn't there. In one way, if it turned into anger, then so be it. At least anger had some strength about it, not like crying and being upset, which to me was weakness. I'd be taught that as a boy. To quote my dad, once when I was a young man when I asked him for support with my mental health, he said, 'You're a man!' Basically, get on with it was what he meant, so that's what I tried to do: get on with it. To preserve the front that I was putting on, my answers would certainly have remained clipped when others asked me how I was doing.

'Fine, thanks,' was still my most regular chant. 'I'm okay,' was a close second. These were the same chants I'd used when people used to ask me how Michelle and the Bears were when she was pregnant. 'Fine thanks' and 'I'm okay' covered everything.

People didn't want to hear that I was a broken man, that I had no idea how to grieve, no idea how me and Michelle were every going to return to any type of normality, no idea how I was gonna stop the negative, self-destructive thoughts that barely left my head. I couldn't let it out. It was too much for me to handle, so I wasn't going to spill my guts on anyone else. It was all just too much. Besides all that, I was spent more time worrying about how they were feeling, rather than concerning myself over my own feelings.

My treatment with the psychologist continued by telephone. I was four years into treatment by now. We did talk about the Bears, of course, but I still didn't want to go there. I wanted to keep it as general as I could – not easy when being questioned by a psychologist, but I didn't want to give in to him either. Well, give in to myself.

Keeping my grief in was a function that kept me safe from facing what I was feeling and the risk of crumbling. I thought that burying it deep was the way forward in the hope that one day it would just decide to go away because it wasn't getting the attention it needed. *Keep busy* was my own chant to myself. I started to question the point of even having treatment anymore.

It had served me well this far, I guess. Without it, I would have been in the grave myself by now – but wasn't that where I really wanted to be now anyway? What was the point? What was the point of working hard to get better when it seemed there was just more and more shit being thrown at me? Was it really worth it if the outcome of my life was still gonna be full of trauma?

The pull to my old ways was there, tugging away at me. It would have been so easy just to say, 'Fuck it! I've had enough!' and just walk away, give in and go back to how I was before treatment, full of self-destructive behaviours and attitudes, back to just surviving and hoping that someone would end my life for me because I was such a coward and couldn't do it myself.

Treatment before any of this had happened with Michelle's pregnancy or the Bears being born had been hard enough. It had already been putting Michelle under stress, as well as the shit that I was having to face from my past week in, week out. Then there was the cost of every session.

When was I ever gonna cop a break, eh? Never. That's how it felt. Never. I'd completely fucked my life up so far and now I was reaping the rewards. What a fucking idiot I was to think that the rewards would fall in my favour. Who was I trying to kid! I'd been a bastard, and now this was my karma. It might just be better for me to get up and go, save Michelle from any more misery. She'd married me and vowed to be with me for life, but this was no life. We were living a hell together that was crucifying both of us.

I loved and cared for her so deeply, and yet couldn't bear to be around her at times. When I looked at her I saw pain and anguish and I didn't want her reminding me that I felt that way too. I had no idea how this was all gonna go.

46

Within days of Dana's funeral, Michelle's parents were moving house, and out of the home that Michelle had lived in for most of her childhood. This offered her a bit of a distraction and purpose and I was glad. Everyone was still so full of grief, but being active and having a purpose to get up out of bed and do something other than just grieve was a relief.

I'd worked through the night on the doors the night before, so I wasn't helping, but Michelle did. As much as I'd have been willing to help, I was glad that I didn't have to see people and for them to see me. I didn't want to mix with people who knew the details of what I'd been through, and Michelle's family did. They were grieving, too, and looking at them was like looking at Michelle in a way. Everyone that knew reminded me that I knew, too.

Now we had a grave to visit, as well. The Bears were buried amongst other babies that hadn't made it. I didn't want to go. It reminded me that they were in there, buried in their little coffins and that I couldn't get them out.

I guess I called at the grave out of a sense of duty as their dad, but I'd stand there for a minute and then I'd be gone again. As long as it was tidy – my purpose for going – then I'd done my bit. Being there made me feel more open, vulnerable almost. I didn't want the label of the dad that had dead children. If I ever got to the grave and I could see other people around, I'd stay in the car until they were gone. I didn't want them looking at me. I didn't want their looks of sadness as they saw me walk towards where all the dead babies were buried.

I know you might think that people wouldn't be looking, but they were. It was bad enough them knowing that I was in the baby part of the graveyard, let alone if they saw the plaque at the head of the Bears' grave that told that two babies were buried there together. I didn't want theirs or anybody's sympathy.

In fairness, Michelle wasn't obsessed about going to the graveyard either. She said that she remembered a friend of hers whose child had died, and she'd become pretty much obsessed with constantly visiting the grave, much to the detriment of her life and the lives of people around her. Having seen how destructive it had been, Michelle didn't want to be the obsessive, grieving mother herself.

We never went together to the Bears' grave. I couldn't go with Michelle; I had to go on my own. Sure, she wanted me to go with her, but I just couldn't. It would be too much. I'd have to relive the moments that we'd stood there together before, the days we'd buried our Little Bears. I didn't want to do that, so I never said yes to her. She went on her own, I went on my own. That was just the way it was gonna be, and I couldn't see that ever changing. I was right. To this day, I can count on one hand the amount of times that we've visited the grave together.

November quickly turned into December and the whole world was getting ready for Christmas, except us. Well, that's how it felt. Myself and Michelle had decided that we weren't gonna buy each other presents like we normally would. It just didn't feel like the right thing to do.

Besides, we were planning to head off to Ireland for a short break, just the two of us, once the New Year was out of the way, as Michelle's family had clubbed together to buy us a ferry ticket. Such unexpected generosity; we couldn't have afforded to go if they hadn't. We had a place to stay once we were over there, so there'd be no additional accommodation costs, just living expenses. Instead of trying to buy presents for each other that neither of us felt like buying or wanted to receive, we'd put the money towards our spending money for Ireland. We were being realistic, but it also gave us an excuse not to have to go out shopping to buy stuff or pretend that we were happy to do it.

Michelle's brother and his wife had asked us if we'd like to go and have Christmas dinner with them. In fact, all of Michelle's family had said that we'd be welcome at any of their houses. It felt like going to Paul and Margaret's would be what we both could cope with. They'd been so involved with everything to do with the Bears that it felt easy to be with them, and anyway, they only lived up the road, and we could come and go with ease without feeling like we were letting anyone down.

They had four young children of their own, and we knew that their Christmas excitement and joy would keep us going and get us

183

through. Michelle's parents' new house was not too much further along from Paul's either, and they were gonna pop in to see us all at some point, so there was no pressure to go Christmas 'house hopping' to other people's houses, like Christmas Day can sometimes turn out like. They were coming to us.

As Christmas approached, everyone was consumed with Yuletide spirit when I was on the doors. Office parties were in full swing and there was merriment everywhere you looked. I acted like I was part of it when I needed to with the customers, but inside I was numb. I didn't even want to feel the hurt anymore. When the hurt stated to push itself up, I did my best to curb it with numbness, to completely disassociate myself from it, like I was looking in at myself from another body. It allowed me to function, or rather, to act like I was functioning would be a better description.

It was a way of coping of burying how I felt about the experiences I'd been through. I wasn't sure how long it was gonna last or how long I'd be able to keep up the pretence, but for now it was doing the job and I wasn't about to let go of it. There was part of me that wanted stuff to kick off when I was on the doors, just so that I had some sort of outlet to get the adrenalin pumping and release some of my pent-up tension.

Punters kicking off definitely did that. No bouncer really wants things to kick off – well, the good ones anyway – as it can get dangerous, but I had a need to open one of my escape hatches and let out some steam. Knowing Les was with me prevented me from acting up or overreacting. I wasn't gonna put him in jeopardy. Of course, it did kick off at times, and it was my job to sort it, which I did, but it didn't kick off because of me.

Then it was Christmas Day. Less than a month after Dana's funeral. Me and Michelle wished each other 'Happy Christmas', but it was accompanied by sadness and tears that I didn't want to see or feel myself, but that was impossible. There was no Christmas spirit in our house, no decorations, nothing. It was hard to imagine that Christmas could be any other way from here on in. Every Christmas we'd have to remember that the Bears weren't gonna be with us, that we'd never get to wrap and open presents with them, play games and wear paper hats from Christmas crackers.

Going to Paul and Margaret's would be a relief. We were gonna visit the grave before we went, separately, of course. I went while Michelle was getting ready, and then she went herself. It wasn't something that we had a great lot of conversation about. What was there to say? For me, the less said the better.

As you'd imagine, with four kids Paul and Margaret's house was a hive of excitement when we arrived. Father Christmas had been and the buzz from the children was amazing. It was time to put on my best face and try and join in, and to their credit they did make it easy for us.

I'm sure there'd been conversation before we arrived about how we might be – I'm sure the kids had been a bit prepped, as well – but to be honest it was great just being there, hard, but great. There were moments of sadness where all of us felt the loss of the Bears, but they passed, and we all got on with what we were there to do. Whether we were all pretending or not, I don't know. My life was one big pretend at that time, so I'm guessing we were, or at least me and Michelle were. The sense of anxiety that grief grabs hold of was still there, but there was definitely some sense of relief at having a day that wasn't like all the others. It was definitely not quite what Christmas had been in past years, but for a short time we weren't immersed in the grief that we felt.

We may not have been immersed, but as soon as we were home again it was difficult not to want to wallow again, not for wallowing's sake but because that was just how we felt. I couldn't wait for the bloody Christmas season shit to be over.

We popped in to see Michelle's parents on Boxing Day. Some of Michelle's family were going, too, so it got another meeting out of the way, each a step further away from everyone having to pussyfoot round us a bit. The fact that Michelle's family was full of young kids was a help. They distracted everyone and entertained us.

Having babies around was less simple; Michelle had a niece and nephew who had been born in June and October respectively. I don't think I held either baby after the Bears died. I couldn't bear it if people were watching how I did it or scrutinising my emotions it. It almost felt like it would be one of those moments in a room where everything would go quiet and faces would turn and stare at me, with glares of, 'Look at him holding someone else's baby,' and 'I wonder if he wishes that it was his own.' I was second guessing everything, not wanting to put myself back in the spotlight for any reason, so I didn't do it. I looked on from afar.

I know that Michelle had had a conversation with her sister about other people's babies. It is a common thing that women who have lost children to want to hold and sometimes take other mothers' babies to replace their own. Thankfully, Michelle's mindset wasn't like mine. She loved her baby niece and nephew because they were who they were. They weren't hers and she didn't want them to be. Michelle wanted her own family, to hold her own baby. Sitting there in a room with them, it did make me think about all the chances that the Bears would miss out on. They'd never play with their cousins and be with them growing up. They'd never know what if felt like to be part of a big family and the rewards that that brought. They'd never know anything, because they just weren't here and weren't ever going to be.

47

Back before Christmas, Michelle had filled a photo album with the photographs of the Bears – the few that we had – and all the bits and pieces they had were put in a memory box. The album also had things like their birth certificates, death certificates, baptismal certificates, funeral booklets, our cards from the funeral and so on.

Michelle was genuinely frightened she'd start to forget the Bears. Their memories were so limited and so precious to us and I got what she meant. People were already starting to avoid talking about them for fear they might upset us, so would simply ask how we were and leave it at that.

But the Bears were real human beings! I'd held and kissed them both! It would be unimaginable in normal circumstances to not talk to a mum or dad about their children, especially when they're babies. Yet actually Bears – what they were like, what I remembered – were never a topic of conversation as the weeks went on.

People were scared to go there and as much as I wanted them to reassure me they still lived on in people's memory, I couldn't let myself start chatting about them anyway. It was so conflicting. Part of me was glad that they weren't the topic of conversation anymore and part of me worried that not just me, but other people, would start forgetting about them, too.

Of course people weren't doing that. There was just a big elephant in the room, and no one knew whether it was okay to talk about the Bears or not. 'Not' won most of the time. Even if they did come up in conversation in a room of people, there'd be a sudden hush where people almost waited with bated, strained breath to see what the answer would be from me or Michelle. Obviously, it was hard to talk about them, not like it should have been. I was such a proud dad and missed them so deeply, but talking about them just went against what my mind and guts were telling me.

Looking back, people, particularly those who were not necessarily close to either off us, but wanted to sympathise in some way, would make so-called comforting comments like: 'They're in a better place now.'

Were they fuck! The better place would have been here with their mum and dad, and family.

187

I know people meant well, and often didn't know what to say, so they came out with standard lines, but for fuck's sake! I even remember an incident where a family friend of Michelle's parents blatantly ignored her when they met up in a group because he didn't know what to say.

Well, blatantly ignoring someone is not the way to go, either! It made Michelle feel excluded, embarrassed and even more vulnerable than she already was.

48

Normally for New Year, we'd either go up north together, or I'd spend New Year's Eve in Birmingham with Michelle and drive up on my own to see my friends on New Year's Day morning. Where I come from, New Year's Day itself is a bigger celebration New Year's Eve. Everyone who lived away would be home, and everyone that still lived there would be out, so the craic and the banter from everyone was brilliant. I got to see so many people that I wouldn't have otherwise seen.

This year I wasn't gonna go. I couldn't and didn't want to leave Michelle, and frankly, I didn't feel like facing so many people from home, some who would know what I'd just been through and some not. It was safer to stay where I was. I could work on the doors, keep busy and New Year would pass.

At midnight, Michelle and I just held each other and lay in bed. 2003 was over. I was leaving the worst year of my life behind, yet wanting to hold on to it at the same time. 2004 had arrived, a new start, a new beginning for me and Michelle. 2004 had to be a better year, it just had to be.

As planned, a few days after New Year, myself and Michelle went to Ireland. We drove to Holyhead where we got the ferry. It was so much better to be out of the rut that we were in at home, and such a relief to be away from everyone. Now we didn't have to think about how we should act, how we should look, who knew and who didn't. There was some sort of pressure taken away. Not grief, not really, just a sense of freedom from what our norm had become.

We didn't do a lot. We walked along beaches, we did a bit of wondering around the shops, we watched films in front of an open fire and we ate out sometimes. The weather was pretty shocking, but we didn't care. It was the first time in ages that I felt like I wanted to be around Michelle – I mean genuinely – without having the urge to walk away from her. She was more relaxed away from home, too. Being somewhere else really helped, seeing different beautiful views and getting bashed by the sea breezes was exactly what we needed.

Nothing was going to take our grief away, we knew that only too well; but the peace and tranquillity that the break offered us definitely gave us some respite. I was dreading going back home. I knew what we were gonna step back into and I just wanted to stay in the cocoon that we'd created away from home.

The world had continued to spin and move on when we returned home from Ireland. As soon as we got back, I finally attended the training that would enable me to start my new job with the Royal Mail as one of their security drivers – delivering and collecting huge amounts of money. This new distraction, and change in faces and conversation, was what I thought I needed and I was able to falsely engage and 'forget' for a few hours.

None of the people I worked with knew about what I'd just been through, so it was easier to act normal around them. There were no expectations and no glares.

Of course, I wasn't normal at all. The trauma of the pregnancy, the birth and then the deaths of the Bears was still so raw, and I continued to blame myself. I still felt that it was my fault that the Bears had died, and it was my fault that I'd caused so much grief, pain and sorrow to Michelle and everyone else.

I felt detached from myself. It was easier that way. I could be sitting in conversation around a table and seem engaged, but all the time my mind was elsewhere. I'd smile and nod and do all the right things, but I'd be somewhere else.

My beaming smile became such a defence mechanism – in truth it always had been for me, ever since I was a kid – but I was aware that I was using it to keep people at bay. If people saw me with a smile on my face, they'd think that I was okay and let me get on with whatever I was doing. I was a master at it.

I couldn't even phone my mate, Michael. I just couldn't physically pick up the phone and dial his number. Mentally, I couldn't contemplate what I'd say, what we'd talk about or whether I'd be upbeat enough to even hold a conversation.

I hated myself for what had happened and I thought the world hated me back because of it. But what I thought and felt, to the outside world, was invisible, it was all going on inside. Sure, people might have seen a dad who had just buried two of his children, but past that? No one knew how damaging my thoughts were about myself.

Talking Michelle about it in much detail wasn't gonna happen, either. I knew that I should have, but again, the words just wouldn't come out, and anyway, I was worried that if they did, they'd all come out wrong. When I looked at Michelle, she looked fragile and vulnerable in so many ways. I knew a part of her had died with the Bears, as it had in me, but I did wonder if I'd ever get her back again, if she'd get me back again, if anything would feel right again.

What was certain was that we loved each other very much, and wanted things to work, but there was no way of knowing whether love would be good enough, or strong enough, to see us through. We'd always been really good at being able to decipher and separate the love that we had for each other from the shit that we'd gone through already – before the Bears – but there was no way of knowing if we'd be able to continue doing that, or wanting to do it.

How easy it would have been to have thrown in the towel. This wasn't an option I wanted to take, but I knew it was hovering around. I could see myself going down the road of choosing loneliness and mental isolation as a safety mechanism that was just as harmful as helpful.

As distracting as my new job was, I was always hyper alert. I functioned well and tattooed a smile on my face, but I knew that I was mentally fragile underneath.

There were surveillance reports sent daily informing us about possible security risks – potential armed robberies, really – and I remember that, like when I was on the doors, I had a bit of a blasé attitude to the dangers to myself and a flicker of 'bring it on then' about me. Was it that I was gunning for a fight or a showdown? Or was it that I'd just had enough and didn't give a shit if something happened to me?

I'd felt self-destructive many times in my life and part of me could feel the remnants of the young sixteen-year-old inside me revving up, the lad who tried to drive his motorbike into the side of a wagon, hoping that it'd bring an end to everything.

Company rules said that helmets had to be worn for safety, but I never wore mine. Speaks volumes, doesn't it? I'd hear of other vehicles being attacked and wonder why it couldn't have been mine. I didn't live in the thoughts, but they were certainly there.

191

When I was able to cast them aside for a short time, the work routine did keep me going and I did enjoy the banter with the lads. The continuous change of scene driving around in security trucks helped to keep my mind busy, if for only short spells. It kept me free from the destructive, dark thoughts that were still constantly trying to creep in.

49

I'd always loved contact sport and self-defence and it became a crucial part of my life around now. I'd done boxing and kick boxing growing up and right into my twenties, and it had been a godsend then as it was to become now. People sometimes underestimate the benefits of physical exercise on your mental health. As bad as my mental health had been my whole life, I know it would have been a whole lot worse without physical exercise. Going somewhere and getting my aggression out in some sort of controlled manner was always my go-to strategy, and I'd never needed it more than I did now.

Before Michelle had become pregnant with the Bears, I'd been training under my good friends Andy and Sharon Hopwood in their dojo in Bromsgrove. It wasn't the nearest training to me by any means, but I knew that going there to them was right for me. Just the feeling of walking through the doors gave me a sense of satisfaction and belonging, whether it be for a class or a one-to-one session.

Even during Michelle's pregnancy, I'd been going across to Bromsgrove to train. It was another way to occupy myself, let off steam and give myself a mental break with everything that was going on at that time. It gave me a chance to clear my head for a bit. Andy and Sharon were great; they'd ask how things were but not dwell on it. I knew that they were there for me if I needed them and that suited us all fine. I was hoping that within about a year I'd be able to go for my black belt, so the training wasn't easy.

Then the Bears died. Training took a back seat, and my mental and physical health with it. I knew I wanted to get back into training, and that I needed to for my own wellbeing. However, the thought of having to walk into the dojo for the first time since I'd lost the Bears was excruciating.

I remember driving there – about a forty-minute drive – with my hands gripping the steering wheel like it would escape from me should I let it go. The closer I go to Bromsgrove, the worse my breathing became and I was taking huge gulps of breath into my lungs by the time I was parking up. I felt sick, so sick that I thought I'd vomit when I opened the car door. I wanted to walk in and for there to be no fuss made. I wanted to train, not be stared at as the grieving dad. Because these people meant something to me, I guess I was worried that I'd break down in front of them and cause a scene – the last thing that I'd want to do.

Andy and Sharon were both there when I arrived. The first thing that they both did was give me a hug – a hug that said a thousand words and meant the world to me.

'Welcome back, Gaz,' was all that was needed.

Then it was straight on to what lay ahead in the session, accompanied by the usual banter and piss-taking.

I worked to capacity in all my training sessions. It was regular for me to push myself so hard that I'd have to leave the gym to go and vomit. It was my parameter – weird, I know – but when the sick came, I knew that I'd worked hard enough. Sometimes I'd push myself so hard a second time that I'd have to go and be sick again. Not the best way to train, but it was what I did. Training to such an extent meant that not only was I pushing myself to my capacity, but doing so released all sorts of mental shit that I was hiding within.

Every move, hit, throw, whatever, would allow more to unhinge and break away from me. Even the vomiting was key; the very act of doing it released the pressure and pent-up emotions that caused my stomach to churn constantly. It does sound extreme, even as I write this, and it probably looked pretty extreme to those watching on, but it was what I needed to do. It was pure, self-indulgent clear-out time.

It was time away from home, away from grief, and away from my treatment, which I continued to wonder about, and doubt. Was it making me worse or better? Destroying me or healing me? It was time away from reality, which was essential for me. No matter how exhausted the training and the vomiting made me feel, the exhaustion came with a sense of ease, accomplishment and relief.

50

I wonder if this has ever happened to you. When you fancy a new car, whatever make and model you choose you have that picture in your head, and suddenly you see loads and loads of them driving round. It's like your eyes have been suddenly opened and you notice them even though they've obviously been driving around before.

Well, I felt like that. Everywhere I looked there were pregnant women, buggies, dads holding babies and groups of people meeting up with their babies. It all seemed to be everywhere I looked.

Why hadn't I really noticed it before? Every time, it gave me a pain in my guts that reminded me that my girls were dead. It was something that I'd have to try and switch off from or not go there, or else I'd be feeling that way throughout the day, and there was enough of feeling sick to the pit of my stomach without adding to it.

When there's an event in your life, usually big or significant, it becomes a landmark, a point of reference that everything else is then levered against. I'll try and explain what I mean.

People say things like:

'Yeah, that was before we got married... after we got married...'

'That happened at my old job when I worked for...'

'That was around the time I finished uni...'

'We were doing that before you were born...'

The list could go on. I hope you catch my drift.

I had a new and very much unwanted landmark. For me, it was now gonna be 'Before the Bears died...' and 'After the Bears died...'

I didn't want it, but it was there and my brain did it automatically. I thought about them constantly, so the pole of reference was played out many times a day. To this day, when Michelle and I are chatting, it is still a reference point. We have many more, but we still use it. It has become a bit broader, if you like. 'Before the Bears died' has become 'Before the Bears,' and the same with 'After the Bears'. The word 'died' is left unsaid.

At home, we tried as best we could to function and bring back some thread of normality through the grief. At the end of that month, we had my birthday coming up, which was an opportunity or a reason, to make ourselves do something that was joyful.

We'd always enjoyed going out for food together, so we said we'd go for a meal and get ourselves dressed up a bit for the occasion. I'm not much of a 'dresser-upper' at the best of times, so getting a bit dressed up for me is literally putting on a pair of smart jeans and a decent T-shirt or shirt. We weren't talking black tie dressing up, but dressing up nevertheless.

It went against the emotional grain a bit, but we knew at some stage that we would have to start doing 'normal' things again, the things that we enjoyed doing together, if life was ever going to settle back into any kind of normality and we were going to survive as a couple. The freedom of being away in Ireland had definitely started the ball rolling, so going out here was another step forward: out into the public arena, but local.

As much as you know that parts of you are still just functioning, functioning is better than autopilot, and so a step above and further towards the light at the end of the tunnel. The tunnel may be long and appear never ending, but the more you walk through it, even if you're nowhere near the end, the brighter the tunnel starts to become. This is where I wanted to be. I had no idea whether the tunnel of darkness that I was walking through would end, but I wanted it to get lighter and brighter with time, so that I could look back at the darkness within it and know how far I'd come.

Off we went to a restaurant to celebrate my birthday, and we acted like any other couple having an evening out. We ate nice food and held hands as we walked. It felt good to be doing something different yet familiar.

Michelle was taking maternity leave until Easter, so she had more time on her hands than me. She'd been a previous member of a gym up the road from us, but had suspended her membership while she was pregnant with the Bears. It was a positive step for her to reinstate that membership and go for a swim every morning – something she'd always loved – after she'd dropped me at work for an early shift.

Her best friend also owned a café that opened early, so she'd often go down there and spend time with her mate. The presence of her family and friends around her kept her going and gave her purpose. Then she'd collect me from work in the evening and we'd catch up on our day. I'd relay the banter from the blokes or stories of the exploits in the van, and she'd fill me in on the gossip she'd heard. The chat was easy and light when we were together and there were no outside pressures.

Home began to feel more familiar, too. When it was just the two of us or we were around familiar people that we felt comfortable with, there was a feeling that life was going to go on and that we'd be all right. When that 'all right' would actually come was anyone's guess, but there was hope, and hope was a feeling that I'd held and lost in such a traumatic way, but that was now showing glimpses of returning.

It wasn't even a conscious thought most of the time, but I'd catch myself beginning to see it in so many ways. Hope for the future, mine and Michelle's, one day we would be able to see more light in the tunnel; hope that we'd be able to have more, healthy children together and become the family that we'd wanted so much.

It was with this sense of hope that we began to talk seriously about trying for another baby. We'd had the conversation on and off over many months, to be fair. We both knew that we wanted to try for a baby, but were understandably scared of doing so, and sometimes upset at the prospect of it, as if we were pushing the Bears aside and moving on.

Of course we weren't; nothing could be further from the truth. We knew that in reality the emotions were still raw and real. It was not something that we were going to do lightly. There were so many what-if scenarios, emotional ones and practical ones.

We were also conscious of how long it had taken Michelle to get pregnant with the Bears, so we were expecting a long journey ahead, but as the weeks passed, we talked about it more and more, and within us both that sense of hope increased.

Our Little Bears were still so at the forefront of our thinking and the traumatic events that we'd been through, but we knew that we wanted to have another child, a child that would have two older sisters in heaven to look after them: sisters we would talk about and relay stories of our memories of them, who might look like their younger brother or sister, and give us times when we'd be able to say:

'Look at his/her nose, it's just like Dana's.'

'He/she looks so much like Alana when he/she is sleeping.'

The Bears may not be physically with us ever again, but they would never, ever leave us. With that hope in mind, I tried to look forward to the future, to the day when Michelle would say: 'I'm pregnant.'

On 16th March 2004, she did.

Acknowledgements

There are so many people I need to thank, but the people who mean so much in my life apart from my wife and children are my good friends. They will never know how much they all mean to me. I am truly blessed to have them in my life. Although they are friends and I never take friendship lightly, they are family to me. I truly believe that if my good friends hadn't been in my life growing up, I wouldn't have still been around, telling part of my story today. I want to thank every one of them: Michael Guthrie, Chris Lambert (Basha), Robert Norris (Jeeky), Stephen Coulter (Coulta), Anthony Fergie (Ants), Brian Morton and Sean Simpson (RIP).

I would also like to thank Michelle's family and friends for all their endless, continuous support and kindness before and after our little girls died, along with Jimmy White, Glen Gillam and Les Goldingay (RIP).

I would also like to thank the people of Berwick-upon-Tweed and across Birmingham who have supported me on so many occasions to raise charity money through my many exploits for the Fetal Medicine Department at Birmingham Woman's Hospital. A total of over £30,000 has been raised over the years, which I know has helped lots of families going through similar experiences.

I would also like to thank Andy and Sharon Hopwood from the Hopwood Fight Centre. I will always be thankful that I could escape to them, away from all that was going on round me.

I would like to thank every medical member of staff that supported us all along the journey: City Hospital, Birmingham; Birmingham Women's Hospital; Shrewsbury Royal Hospital; and Birmingham Children's Hospital. I would particularly like to thank the staff from the Fetal Medicine Department at Birmingham Woman's Hospital, truly special people in their field: Professor Mark Kilby, Veronica Donavan OBE, Helen Baker, Nia Carnevale, Ruth Kirchmeier and Sandie Smith.

I would like to thank Jack O'Hara for taking my thoughts regarding the design of the front cover and running with it. Such talent! Couldn't have asked for more.

Michelle was invaluable when it came to putting my story into words. I would also like to thank Peter Jones for his patience and kindness in helping to edit this book and Becky Chappell for her valued opinions along the way.